A

WOMAN'S
Guide to
FASTING

A
WOMAN'S
Guide to
FASTING

LISA E. NELSON

BETHANY HOUSE PUBLISHERS
a division of Baker Publishing Group
Minneapolis, Minnesota

© 2011 by Lisa E. Nelson

Published by Bethany House Publishers
11400 Hampshire Avenue South
Bloomington, Minnesota 55438
www.bethanyhouse.com

Bethany House Publishers is a division of
Baker Publishing Group, Grand Rapids, Michigan

Printed in the United States of America

Page 157 is a continuation of the copyright page.

Library of Congress Cataloging-in-Publication Data

Nelson, Lisa E.
A woman's guide to fasting / Lisa E. Nelson.
    p. cm.
    Summary: "A practical resource for Christian women who want to practice the spiritual discipline of fasting. Key topics include how to prepare physically and spiritually for different types of fasts, what to expect during the fast, and how to reintroduce food"—Provided by publisher.
    Includes bibliographical references (p.   ).
    ISBN 978-0-7642-0902-4 (pbk. : alk. paper) 1. Christian women—Religious life. 2. Fasting—Religious aspects—Christianity. I. Title.
BV4527.N378 2011
248.4'7—dc23   2011019420

Emphasis in Scripture shown by italics is the author's.

The information provided herein should not be construed as a health-care diagnosis, treatment regimen, or any other prescribed health-care advice or instruction. The information is provided with the understanding that the publisher is not engaged in the practice of medicine or any other health-care profession and does not enter into a health-care practitioner/patient relationship with its readers. The publisher does not advise or recommend to its readers treatment or action with regard to matters relating to their health or well-being other than to suggest that readers consult appropriate health-care professionals in such matters. No action should be taken based solely on the content of this publication. The information and opinions provided herein are believed to be accurate and sound at the time of publication, based on the best judgment available to the author. However, readers who rely on information in this publication to replace the advice of health-care professionals, or who fail to consult with health-care professionals, assume all risks of such conduct. The publisher is not responsible for errors or omissions.

Cover design and photography by Andrea Boven Nelson

12   13   14   15   16   17   7   6   5   4   3

Contents

CHAPTER 1

What Is Fasting?

I have come that they may have life, and that they may have it more abundantly.

—John 10:10 NKJV

Fasting is amazingly powerful. It is simple, but not easy. Most people can fast successfully with just a little information and encouragement. Let's not make fasting into some impossibly difficult practice reserved for a select few.

The aim of this book is to equip you with practical information about the physical and spiritual aspects of fasting. Why? Because fasting satisfies the desire of our hearts: to know and walk intimately with God.

I was raised Catholic. Because of my strong Catholic faith, I knew that Jesus was the Savior; I just didn't understand that He was *my* Savior. When I was in college, I was invited to an Inter-Varsity Christian Fellowship Bible study on my dorm floor. As

I studied the Bible, my eyes were opened and I came to a saving faith in Jesus Christ.

Catholics fast. While I was Catholic, I fasted on Ash Wednesday and Good Friday, and I fasted from meat on every Friday during Lent. When I stopped worshiping in the Catholic Church, I stopped fasting.

Fifteen years went by and I was steadily growing in faith. I was teaching women's Bible studies and leading prayer. I was a stay-at-home mom with two small children. One day I received a letter from my old boss. We had served together as army JAG officers. I thought the world of him: great leader, good man, excellent officer. He wrote that he had just been diagnosed with stage-4 lung cancer. Forty-eight years old, he had retired only two years previously and had never smoked a day in his life. He knew I was a Christian and asked me to pray for him. He was a lapsed Catholic.

I was getting ready to eat lunch when I got that letter. I was so shocked by the news that I had to read it twice. Tears filled my eyes. Immediately the Lord impressed upon my mind, "Fast and pray." I left the table and walked to my bedroom and started to pray. I understood the Lord was asking me to fast and pray for the rest of that day. I fasted from lunch and dinner. I prayed. I emailed other Christians and asked them to pray. I put him on every prayer chain I knew.

I wrote back and told him I was praying. A few months later he wrote again and thanked me for praying. He said he had reconciled himself with God and regretted neglecting the church. He had surrendered his life to Christ. He especially regretted that his children were not raised in faith and asked me to pray for them. As much as I had prayed for his physical healing, I desired his soul's salvation most of all. I was overjoyed and praised God over and over.

He died a few months later. When I attended his funeral Mass, I felt the Holy Spirit wash over me, assuring me, again, that my boss was now in glory. Outwardly I was calm; inwardly I was floating with joy.

———

When I could look back and analyze that whole experience, I realized:

God initiated the fast.

God empowered my prayer in that fast.

The fast was for only two meals, yet it was powerful and effective.

My faith in God exploded.

I began searching for more information on fasting. I sensed the Lord was leading me to incorporate fasting into my life, but I wasn't sure how. Should I wait for another clear invitation from Him? Should I set up a certain day to fast? I was at a loss. I found Richard Foster's *Celebration of Discipline* and read the chapter on fasting. He wrote about fasting regularly for twenty-four hours each week. Then I came across a passage that has been a useful guide to me ever since: "If our fasting is not unto God, we have failed. Physical benefits, success in prayer, the enduing of power, spiritual insights—these must never replace God as the center of our fasting."[1]

I began to fast once a week over a three-month period. My faith grew. And all these years later, fasting is a vital part of my faith walk with Jesus.

This may sound weird, but fasting is a joy. It reveals my motives and the true condition of my heart. The Word of God nearly leaps off the page when I'm fasting. I hear God so clearly and know His will so plainly that my prayers are powerful and effective. I forgive others and ask for forgiveness. But as useful as fasting is, I don't forget it is merely a tool. I don't love fasting; I love God.

Since that first fast in 1997, God has invited me to fast repeatedly. He has used this simple practice to mature me, to grow me in grace and truth. I have learned to fast for anywhere from a few meals to forty days. I have made mistakes in fasting, and I have had amazing victories in fasting.

I am convinced the Holy Spirit is calling us to a holy and deeper walk of faith. He is inviting us to fast.

FASTING IS A DISCIPLINE

Many of us have come to salvation through Jesus Christ by faith, and we know we're supposed to walk out this salvation by faith. Yet many of us are wondering exactly how to do that. We may have been taught that "faith in action" is believing in and obeying God, but we're just not sure what that looks like in real life. We soon realize we can't overcome sin in our own strength, and at the same time we know that we can't just sit back and wait for God to wave a magic wand, and poof! all our sinful desires are gone. How do we live and walk by faith and not by guilt, wearying works, and failed self-control?

Unsure of what to do, we try a lot of everything: teach Sunday school, help with hospitality, attend prayer services . . . the list grows with our busy Christian activities. We keep hearing that we're set free from the law and that we live by grace, but it doesn't seem to match our busy reality.

After a few years of this, it's easy to question whether that faithful, abundant, overcoming life we read about in Scripture is even possible in our lives. Here's where the Christian disciplines come in. By disciplines, I mean spiritual practices such as prayer, meditation, fasting, Bible study, tithing, and worship.[2] These disciplines are the spiritual tools that God uses to transform us, to bring us to maturity, victory, and freedom in Christ. The disciplines don't accomplish the transformed, abundant life; God does.

These disciplines are not the end in themselves; they are merely the means to the end. The end is the abundant life. Only Jesus provides the abundant life. We can't fast our way into abundance or pray ourselves into freedom. The reason to practice any of these disciplines is that, amazingly, they put us in the position to cooperate with God's internal and eternal work in our souls. Prayer and fasting (and all the other disciplines) are the tools we need to walk out our faith. Faith is a matter of the heart, not a matter of actions. Somehow we get confused and think we can work our way into faith. But it's the opposite; our works must be as a result of our faith ("Show me your faith without deeds, and I will show you my faith by my deeds," James 2:18). The disciplines help strengthen our faith.

It's Like This

Think of it this way. Let's say it's time to get your hair cut, or worse, it's past due and you are thinking of doing something drastic. You are ready for change. You are desperate for change. And it's time to put your hair in the hands of a true professional.

This stylist knows exactly what's best for your hair texture and face shape. She may tell you that you need to let those bangs grow out—a months-long process. She may tell you that you need to cut several inches of hair off. Or that your hair color is wrong, and worse, it is making you look old and tired.

She starts her work. Once in that chair, you may need to lean back for a shampoo. You may need to lean forward to get a short haircut in the back. You may need to close your eyes while bangs are trimmed or hair spray is applied. You may need to sit under the dryer while the color sets. You may even need to hold the little permanent rods and hand them up as the stylist rolls your hair and squirts ice-cold, smelly goop all over your head. You may need to hold a towel over your face to protect your eyes from the relaxing chemicals. You may need to sit still while extensions are weaved in. For hours. Sometimes you need to hold on tight to the chair while the stylist is blow-drying your hair straight up from the roots. And then, finally, you're twirled around to face the mirror. You love it! The stylist has completely transformed your hair. You are beautiful.

Did she do this without your cooperation? Did she wave her magic scissors over your head and transform your hair while you just sat there?

The disciplines are your way of cooperating with God while He transforms your eternal soul.

WHAT IS FASTING?

First, what fasting is not: It's not giving up all food or certain foods for a certain length of time. Merely "not eating" is dieting, or worse, starvation—it is not fasting. Fasting is a spiritual tool for spiritual growth. It is a wholehearted desire to know God and to seek Him. Fasting is giving up something perfectly good and acceptable because you want God more. It is a spiritual discipline with a physical act.

The traditional biblical fast is twenty-four hours with no food—liquids only—starting at sundown and ending the following sundown. The Greek word for fasting in the New Testament is *nesteuo*: to abstain from food. The Hebrew word in the Old Testament is *tsoom*: to cover over the mouth, to fast. You can fast from things such as TV, the Internet, or shopping, and if a food fast won't work for you, these may be great options.

This book is focused on fasting from food. However, the point is less about what you're giving up and more about why you're giving it up.

Fasting is declaring that God is more important than the good food you eat, your routines and schedules, your very life. Fasting is a path to authentic humility before God, a time of Spirit-led self-examination. It is a discipline of grace. Sadly, from Old Testament times until today, the practice of fasting has often been misused as a duty, or an obligation, instead of the spiritual discipline that it is. A clear example of this is seen in Isaiah 58. When the Israelites practiced fasting as a duty, God spoke His disappointment through the prophet Isaiah:

> For day after day they seek me out; they seem eager to know my ways, as if they were a nation that does what is right and has not forsaken the commands of its God. They ask me for just decisions and seem eager for God to come near them. "Why have we fasted," they say, "and you have not seen it? Why have we humbled ourselves, and you have not noticed?" *Yet on the day of your fasting, you do as you please* and exploit all your workers. Your fasting ends in quarreling and strife, and in striking each other with wicked fists. You cannot fast as you do today and expect your voice to be heard on high. Is this the kind of fast I have chosen, only a day for a people to humble themselves? Is it only for bowing one's head like a reed and for lying on sackcloth and ashes? Is that what you call a fast, a day acceptable to the Lord? (vv. 2–5)

True biblical fasting is not about the external act of not eating; it is about the internal work of the heart seeking hard after God. In this passage, God reveals that fasting while doing what you please (and exploiting others) is no fast at all. Yet God does not leave the Israelites without counsel. He defines an acceptable fast:

Is not this the kind of fasting I have chosen: to loose the chains of injustice and untie the cords of the yoke, to set the oppressed free and break every yoke? Is it not to share your food with the hungry and to provide the poor wanderer with shelter—when you see the naked, to clothe them, and not to turn away from your own flesh and blood? Then your light will break forth like the dawn, and your healing will quickly appear; then your righteousness will go before you, and the glory of the Lord will be your rear guard. Then you will call, and the Lord will answer; you will cry for help, and he will say: Here am I. . . . Your light will rise in the darkness, and your night will become like the noonday. The Lord will guide you always; he will satisfy your needs in a sun-scorched land and will strengthen your frame. (vv. 6–11)

Again, as diligent as the Israelites were about observing the appointed fast days, it was worthless in God's eyes. They had turned fasting into a mere ritual, a selfish act. Acceptable fasting to the Lord is when there is true personal humility and others-oriented living. Then, with a contrite and humble heart, we can call out to the Lord and He will answer, He will guide, He will strengthen.

This idea of fasting out of duty was still alive and well in Jesus' time. When Jesus chastised the Pharisees and the hypocrites for their fasting practices, it was for the same root of legalism:

When you fast, do not look somber as the hypocrites do, *for they disfigure their faces to show others they are fasting. I tell you the truth, they have received their reward in full.* But when you fast, put oil on your head and wash your face, so that it will not be obvious to others that you are fasting, but only to your Father, who is unseen; and your Father, who sees what is done in secret, will reward you. (Matthew 6:16–18)

The Pharisees, like the Israelites in Isaiah's day, had taken a powerful discipline of grace and made it into a legal obligation. The reward for true fasting is the transformational work of God, not a self-satisfied check-in-the-box for following a rule perfectly. The reason to fast is to be changed from our normal state of selfishness that desires the praise of men, into a godly servant, concerned with the things that concern God.

FASTING IN GRACE

True fasting—that is, fasting acceptable to the Lord—always requires humility. Humility is the submission of the heart. It is kicking "self" off of the throne of our lives and choosing God to be the King and Master over self.

Let's say we have the right heart attitude. Now what? What do we do during a fast? How is fasting under grace different from fasting under law?

I mentioned before that the traditional biblical fast is twenty-four hours, liquids only, from sundown to sundown. In grace, a fast might be one meal, two meals, twenty-four hours, juices only, certain foods only, weekly, monthly, or yearly. Because we fast not under a legal obligation but under a heart's cry for God, God directs our fasts in individual and personal ways.

Liquids-Only Fast

What does a liquids-only fast consist of? How much should I drink? Does liquid mean water only? Can it mean coffee? Diet Coke?

Fasting under grace is defined by the heart, not by the liquid. I will discuss the details of good liquids in chapters 4 and 5, but for those who are eager for details, here is a quick overview of a twenty-four-hour, liquids-only fast.

I spent a year fasting for twenty-four hours each week. I rarely ever had water only. I'm a tea drinker, so while fasting I drank tea—that is, hot tea with milk. Sometimes I put honey in my tea. I also drank fruit juices, especially cranberry juice. Usually I would dilute the cranberry juice with water or seltzer water and drink a large twenty-ounce glass of it. If I were a coffee drinker, I would have had coffee. I recognize that coffee is a diuretic, so if you drink coffee, please be especially careful to drink other, non-diuretic liquids. For serious coffee drinkers, going without caffeine will result in a horrible headache—and may make fasting feel too painful. I like a Diet Coke once in a while, and if I wanted a Diet Coke, I drank it. Sometimes I had broth.

Drink more than you think you'll need. Because you're not getting the liquids found in foods, you'll need to be vigilant about drinking liquids. Don't wait until you are thirsty. Drink when you would be having a meal and drink in between. Your urine should be light colored. If it is dark, you're not getting enough liquid. If your stomach is rumbling, drink. Also, don't gulp. Drink slowly to avoid hiccups.

I have nothing against a twenty-four-hour water-only liquid fast. My concern with fasting only with water is twofold. First, because I can find no biblical requirement for water only, why should we make such a requirement? Since fasting is not about the liquid or the food but about the heart, how does requiring water as the only acceptable liquid result in fasting under grace? And worse, if we make water the only acceptable liquid, couldn't we then fall into the trap of judging another's fast by what she drinks? Or maybe puff ourselves up with our "superior" water-only fasting? We would then reduce fasting to a physical act to be measured and compared, just as the hypocritical Pharisees did. Second, water-only fasting provides no energy. The reality of our busy lives makes following the discipline of fasting difficult.

Adding rules, and subtracting energy, makes it nearly impossible for the woman who desires to incorporate this discipline into her life. A little honey, sugar, caffeine, or fruit juice may spell the difference between pursuing God and His righteousness and giving up in exhaustion.

Fasting is hard enough, why make it even harder with rules and regulations about what is an acceptable liquid? If I drank water only and had a heart like God describes in the previous Isaiah and Matthew passages, what would I have gained? It's not the form of liquid you drink, it's what's in your heart that matters. I have fasted for forty days, liquids only, three times. Yet the one year of weekly fasting was as powerful as any forty-day fast. I remember going to social functions during that year and drinking punch, soda, sweetened iced tea—whatever liquid was available. It was an amazing season of fasting that strengthened my soul and, I believe, was acceptable in the Lord's sight.

Partial Fasts

In fasting, we are submitting our hearts to God as fully as we possibly can. We're holding nothing back in our desire to be changed into overcomers, women who walk by faith and who love deeply. We want to be like Jesus. In fasting under grace, there is no less freedom regarding food than there is regarding liquids.

A standard biblical fast is liquids only; a partial fast is liquids and certain foods only; and an absolute fast is swallowing absolutely nothing. I only mention the absolute fast because it is mentioned in the Bible; I do not recommend it. It is potentially dangerous and not necessary in the normal discipline of fasting. I have sought the Lord in prayer, meditation, study, worship, and fasting for many years. I have fasted for twenty-four hours, two days, three days, seven days, nine days, fourteen days, twenty-one days, thirty days, and forty days. I have fasted liquids-only and partial fasts. I have been transformed and I have seen prayers answered. I have never been called to an absolute fast.

The best known example of a partial fast is described in Daniel 10:3. Daniel writes, "I ate no choice food; no meat or wine touched my lips . . . until the three weeks were over." I like to call this the No Meats, Sweets, or Treats Fast. Maybe you're thinking, *Finally! Here's a fast that's just right for me . . . not so hard.* Don't be fooled. All fasting is hard. Remember, it's not about eating or drinking, but about submitting yourself wholeheartedly to God. As long as we're here on earth, our flesh nature always desires to rule and reign. Any time you are submitting the flesh to the Spirit, it's hard.

No meats, sweets, or treats sounds pretty straightforward, right? Not exactly. Is fish meat? Is pizza a treat? Is Jell-O salad with fruit and mini marshmallows a sweet? The only answer to these questions comes through prayer. Ask the Lord about these sorts of decisions *before* you start any fast. Your treat might be my acceptable food. My sweet might be your acceptable food.

My friend Deb was in charge of planning a large Christian women's conference. The four-day event was a huge responsibility—all done as a volunteer. As the conference date approached, Deb felt a call to fast and pray for the conference. As she sought the Lord about how she could fast and seek His will and His favor for the conference while not neglecting her husband and two boys, she heard an unusual solution. She would fast during the day for the thirty days leading up to the conference while joining her family for dinner each night and meals on the weekend. There were no other restrictions. She could eat whatever they were eating at dinner and on the weekends. In the end, Deb was amazed at the power of the fast. Her prayers were especially effective, and she felt a renewed closeness to God and an amazing peace. The conference itself was nothing less than anointed.

Deb's fast was its own type of partial fast. It wasn't in the mold of Daniel's fast, but it is a perfect example of fasting under grace: "You will seek me and find me when you seek me with all your heart" (Jeremiah 29:13). If you desire to fast, whether partial or liquids only, God will show you how to fast. He may design a fast just for you. Trust Him.

Twenty-Four-Hour Fasts

In Bible times, the Pharisees fasted for twenty-four hours twice each week, traditionally on Mondays and Thursdays. Jesus was not impressed with their amount of fasting. Look at His parable in Luke 18:9–14:

> To some who were confident of their own righteousness and looked down on everybody else, Jesus told this parable: "Two men went up to the temple to pray, one a Pharisee and the other a tax collector. The Pharisee stood by himself and prayed: 'God, I thank you that I am not like other people—robbers, evildoers, adulterers—or even like this tax collector. *I fast twice a week* and give a tenth of all I get.' But the tax collector stood at a distance. He would not even look up to heaven, but beat his breast and said, 'God, have mercy on me, a sinner.' I tell you that this man, rather than the other, went home justified before God. For those who exalt themselves will be humbled, and those who humble themselves will be exalted."

There is no evidence that this tax collector fasted at all. Yet he went away justified before God.

This is an important lesson for us. As fasting becomes more popular with today's Christians, we must watch out for the self-righteousness and pride that so easily slips into our lives. It's tempting to think, *If fasting for twenty-four hours is good, then fasting for forty-eight hours or seventy-two hours or three weeks must be better!* Or, worse, *I am a better Christian because I fast.* Dearest sisters in Christ, I'll say it again: It's not the amount of fasting that matters, it's the heart. A Christian who never fasts but has a humble and contrite heart is more pleasing to God than a Christian who fasts for forty days out of self-righteousness.

I believe that fasting is an amazingly effective discipline to incorporate into our walk of faith. All true fasting, whether partial fasting or liquids-only fasting, is powerful. A twenty-four-hour fast is intense. Really. It's good enough. I am convinced that fasting for more than twenty-four hours at a time should be *only* as a result of a clear calling from the Lord (more about this in the next chapter).

Fasting and Prayer

When we think of fasting, our first thought is usually about giving up eating. The reality is, there is no fasting apart from prayer. As I mentioned before, simply not eating is not fasting. Fasting is abstaining from food, or certain foods, in order to devote ourselves to God more fully. Spending time with God in prayer— not abstaining from eating—is the focus of fasting.

One way to spend time in prayer during a fast is to replace mealtimes with prayer times. You might start a standard twenty-four-hour fast after a light dinner and then, before bed, spend time in prayer. The next morning, start your day with prayer and then pray at what would normally be lunchtime. Finally, just before you end the fast with your dinner meal, pray again.

There are many prayer models and ways to help focus your prayer times. I was taught the ACTS method: Start with Adoration, then Confession, then Thanksgiving, and finally praying for others through Supplication. Another prayer model I've learned is PRAY, which has an additional element not in the ACTS model.

In the PRAY model, we start with Praise, then Repent, then Ask, and finally Yield. I love the Thanksgiving part of ACTS and the Yield part of PRAY. If I could figure out a catchy acronym that included both, I would make a new prayer model! Instead, I use ACTS+Y.

A great way to start every prayer is with adoration and praise. For as many years as I've been praying and interceding, I still catch myself rushing right into the supplication and ask part—or maybe, on a good day, the thanksgiving part. Starting with praise and adoration focuses our minds on God, not on our request or concern. Honestly, it's not like we're ever going to utter one prayer request or cry of the heart that He does not already know (Psalm 139:1–4). Start by inviting God's presence with praising Him for who He is. I have found that praying the Psalms is a great way to focus my praise (and my mind). One of my favorites is Psalm 96. My other favorite praise verse is Revelation 5:12: "Worthy is the Lamb, who was slain, to receive power and wealth and wisdom and strength and honor and glory and praise!" I also find it helpful to pray these Scriptures out loud. Then, my eyes, my mind, and my ears are all engaged in the praise of God.

After we've reminded ourselves about His power, holiness, and glory, it's time to examine ourselves. I often ask God to search me, to reveal my thoughts and show me any offense I've committed (Psalm 139:23–24). If there's something to confess, it will immediately come to mind. There's no need for us to go rooting around, looking for something to confess. Confession is agreeing with God that we've sinned. Repentance is often described as turning from the sin we've just confessed, but that's only half of the story. We must turn *from* the sin and *to* God.

The reason we confess and repent is to grow in faith, not to beat ourselves up with guilt. As Paul wrote, "Godly sorrow brings repentance that leads to salvation and leaves no regret, but worldly sorrow brings death" (2 Corinthians 7:10). After we confess and repent, we have this glorious assurance: "If we confess our sins, he is faithful and just and will forgive us our sins and purify us from all unrighteousness" (1 John 1:9). Praying this Scripture, out loud, is another powerful act. I make this truth my own and pray something like, "Heavenly Father, I have confessed my sin before you. I repent. I am turning to you wholeheartedly. You are faithful. You are just. Thank you for forgiving my sin. Thank you for purifying me from all un-righteousness. In Jesus' name, amen."

After we've been reminded of our sin and God's faithful-ness and forgiveness, how can we not thank Him? The thanks-giving part of the ACTS prayer model is a natural next step. Even if I had nothing to confess (ha!), God's Word commands thanksgiving: "Be joyful always; pray continually, give thanks in all circumstances, for this is God's will for you in Christ Jesus" (1 Thessalonians 5:16–18). This passage does not ask us to be thankful *for* each circumstance. You may be suffering under a very difficult circumstance. The Scripture states that we are to be thankful *in* all circumstances, trusting that God is worthy of thanksgiving in spite of our circumstances (Romans 8:28).

After praise and confession and thanksgiving our hearts are tender. Any wrong motives have been exposed and confessed. Now we're invited to ask—not timidly, but with faith, remember-ing that Jesus, who is seated at the right hand of God, lives to intercede for us: "Let us therefore come boldly to the throne of grace, that we may obtain mercy and find grace to help in time of need" (Hebrews 4:16 NKJV). Now is not the time for pretty words and pious-sounding prayers. Ask. Lay bare your heart's desires. Cry out with confidence. Be brutally honest with God. And then yield.

Yielding is the most important part of praying. It might seem like it's the complete opposite of the bold asking we just did. It's not. It's an even more bold and confident asking. When we yield, we are actually asking for God's will to be done, even if it's not what we want. Powerful pray-ers are powerful because they have learned the secret of yielding. Our best example of yielding is Jesus. Matthew records Jesus' yielded prayer in Gethsemane before His arrest and crucifixion:

> Going a little farther, he fell with his face to the ground and prayed, "My Father, if it is possible, may this cup be taken from me. Yet not as I will, but as you will.". . . He went away a second time and prayed, "My Father, if it is not possible for this cup to be taken away unless I drink it, may your will be done" (Matthew 26:39, 42).

Jesus prayed specifically and boldly. He told God exactly what He wanted; He wanted the cup of suffering and crucifixion to be taken from Him. He was prostrate, on his face, humbled before God. He was without sin. He asked and trusted God for the answer. The answer was no.

Sometimes yieldedness starts in the asking part of our prayer. We may be so overwhelmed by a situation that we don't even know what to ask. We don't know how to pray. We're at a loss for words. We're grieved beyond what we can express. We're broken. Yet when we yield in our brokenness,

> the Spirit helps us in our weakness. We do not know what we ought to pray for, but the Spirit himself intercedes for us through wordless groans. And he who searches our hearts knows the mind of the Spirit, *because the Spirit intercedes for God's people in accordance with the will of God.* (Romans 8:26–27)

Our entire prayer may just be sobbing before the Lord. Or crying out for help.

Prayer is not a monologue; it is a dialogue. Prayer with fasting is a deep dialogue. When we fast and pray, we are openly surrendering to the trustworthiness of God, simply because we know He is trustworthy. We are declaring, on earth and in the heavenlies, that He is good and His will is good. When we fast and pray, we know that God himself is our very great reward! (Genesis 15:1).

FASTING WITH HUMILITY

Humility is both a basis for fasting and a result of fasting. We have to be humble enough to fast in the first place. Then fasting makes us more humble.

I'll just confess that in my normal sinful state, I resist being humble. To humble oneself means to lower in importance, to destroy the independence, power, or will of; to make meek. Many of my fellow sisters have told me they share the same struggle with humility. Oh, we all say that God is in control and trustworthy. But deep down, sometimes we really believe that we alone know what's best for us. The truth is, many of our (my) prayers have been ineffective because we are so busy trying to convince God to see things our way. *Why doesn't He just give us what we want?!*

Here is the importance of humility. It is the yielded portion of prayer lived out. It is the intentional dependence on God. It is dying to self—self-will, self importance. There's nothing harder on this earth. It goes against everything in our sin nature. Without Jesus Christ and the indwelling Holy Spirit, it is impossible. The good news is that we can choose to be humble. We can change our self-reliant, proud attitude and be like Jesus.

In your relationships with one another, have the same mind-set as Christ Jesus: Who, being in very nature God, did not consider equality with God something to be used to his own advantage; rather, he made himself nothing by taking the very nature of a servant, being made in human likeness. And being found in appearance as a man, he humbled himself by becoming obedient to death—even death on a cross! (Philippians 2:5–8)

At its very essence, fasting is about selflessness. Selflessness is the critical component to humility, and humility is the means to being Christlike. And isn't being Christlike the goal of every follower of Jesus Christ? Here is the means—fasting—to reach that end, being transformed into the image and likeness of our Lord and Savior, Jesus.

Humbling ourselves through the discipline of fasting is hard and joyful at the same time. It is hard because humility is the opposite of our innate me-centeredness. It is joyful because we begin to see our sinful nature just when we are perfectly equipped to repent. While we are fasting, our eyes are opened more clearly than ever before. We confess and repent, often with tears, and we are transformed. It is a glorious feeling to overcome a sinful habit. This is the goal of all the disciplines, but fasting is particularly effective at this transformational, overcoming work.

Why is the discipline of fasting so effective? I believe it is the combination of sacrifice, plus devoted prayer, plus humility. It requires more of us physically (not eating), mentally (mindful, focused prayer), and spiritually (others-centered, selflessness, and humility) than any other discipline. This potent combination of intentional physical, mental, and spiritual devotion to God allows an amazing work of the Spirit in our souls. The rewards of fasting are even greater than its sacrifices.

FASTING TO WIN

The army requires all soldiers (even its lawyer soldiers) to run two miles and do push-ups and sit-ups. There was a test on all three events every six months. I am not a runner. I don't like to run. As the physical fitness training (PT) test time approached, I would make myself run so I knew I could pass. I had a friend, Robin, who was also a JAG officer. She would run with me and encourage me to keep running when I wanted to stop and walk. She told me the best running advice she got was from a marathon runner who said he started each marathon slowly and then tapered. In other words, he started slow and then slowed down, but never stopped running. It's good advice for fasting, as well. The important thing is to start and then keep going.

We are running a race that God has laid out for us. Let's run it to win the prize. Let's train ourselves with the discipline of fasting so that we can join Paul and say,

> I have fought the good fight, I have finished the race, I have kept the faith. Now there is in store for me the crown of righteousness, which the Lord, the righteous Judge, will award to me on that day—and not only to me, but also to all who have longed for his appearing. (2 Timothy 4:7–8)

CHAPTER 2

Why Fast?

Be very careful, then, how you live—not as unwise but as wise,
making the most of every opportunity, because the days are evil.
Therefore do not be foolish, but understand what the Lord's will
is. Do not get drunk on wine, which leads to debauchery. Instead,
be filled with the Spirit.

—Ephesians 5:15–18

There are many reasons to fast, and whole books have been written on the spiritual benefits of fasting.[1] The Bible specifically mentions fasting:

To request God's intervention for healing (2 Samuel 12:15–17)

To request God's protection (Esther 4:15–16; Ezra 8:21–23)

To set apart leaders for God's work (Acts 13:2–3)

With the confession of sin (1 Samuel 7:6; Nehemiah 9:1–2; Daniel 9:3, 20)

For humility (Psalm 35:13)

With repentance (Joel 1:13–14; 2:12–15)

When called by a leader (Jonah 3:6–10)

To prepare for ministry (Matthew 4:1–17; Luke 4:1–15)

With mourning (Esther 4:3; Daniel 9:3; 1 Samuel 31:13)

Why might we incorporate twenty-four-hour or longer fasts into our lives today? Let's consider five reasons:

1. Fasting helps us to grow spiritually and overcome sin.
2. Fasting empowers our intercession and petitioning.
3. Fasting prepares us for spiritual warfare.
4. Fasting is an obedience to God's call.
5. Fasting is a response to a crisis in our lives.

PERSONAL SPIRITUAL GROWTH

The goal of spiritual growth is spiritual maturity. In order to be spiritually mature, we need to be filled with the Spirit. To be filled with the Spirit, we need to empty ourselves. And emptying ourselves is another way of saying humbling ourselves. So not only does fasting require humility, it teaches humility.

The essence of spiritual maturity is to love God and to love others. When asked what the greatest commandment was, Jesus answered, "Love the Lord your God with all your heart and with all your soul and with all your mind and with all your strength. The second is this: 'Love your neighbor as yourself.' There is no commandment greater than these" (Mark 12:30–31).

How does the discipline of fasting help us to love God with all our heart, soul, mind, and strength? Actually, how do we love God at all? We love through obedience. Jesus said, "Whoever has my commands and *keeps them is the one who loves me.* The one who loves me will be loved by my Father, and I too will love him and show myself to them" (John 14:21). Jesus modeled this love for us and said, "If you keep my commands, you will remain in my love, *just as I have kept my Father's commands and remain in his love*" (John 15:10). We love God not by a feeling or an emotion; we love God by obedient action.

When we continue in a fast, in spite of our hunger, we prove to ourselves that we can obey God. We show ourselves that we love God more than we love our life. We are fully aware of our will and our desires (to eat!), but we choose to be obedient and not eat.

When the fast is over, the lesson of obedience remains. We understand what Jesus meant when He said, "Whoever wants to be my disciple must deny themselves and take up their cross and follow me. For whoever wants to save their life will lose it, but whoever loses their life for me and for the gospel will save it" (Mark 8:34–35). Practicing the discipline of fasting confirms to our souls that we truly love God and that we can obey Him. Meanwhile, God himself strengthens us to love and obey, "for it is God who works in you to will and to act in order to fulfill his good purpose" (Philippians 2:13). Fasting is one of the tools He uses to work in our souls to will (love) and act (obey) according to His good purpose.

In addition to obedience, our love for God is demonstrated in how we love others. We love others by living an others-focused life. Our natural state is to live a self-focused life. Rick Warren captured this concept in the opening statement of his book *The Purpose-Driven Life*: "It's not about you." Instead, life is all about God and others. Paul describes the others-focused life: "Do nothing out of selfish ambition or vain conceit. Rather, in humility value others above yourselves, not looking to your own interests but each of you to the interests of the others" (Philippians 2:3–4). It's hard to live an others-focused life. We need to train ourselves to consider others and to look to the interests of others. But fasting is a faithful trainer. Fasting opens our eyes to our own selfishness. Fasting teaches us to die to self and be filled with the Spirit.

I'm guessing you have certain triggers that reveal to you how self-focused or others-focused you are. I live just outside of Washington, D.C., recognized as the one of the worst areas for traffic in the country. If I want to know how well I look to the interests of others, I need only get in my car and start to drive. There will certainly be an inattentive driver (cell phone, iPod, or just plain lost). There will certainly be construction on the Beltway. There will certainly be people who need to merge or change lanes. Will I yield to them? Will I share my lane? Will it be all about me? Or will I love my fellow motorists?

You and I desire to obey and love God and love others. Yet time and time again we fall into old patterns of sin. We do not want to sin. We want to obey. We desire more than anything to overcome sin and its stronghold. We're just sick of the cycle of sin and repent and sin again.

Here's the truth: All spiritual victory is a result of obedience. Like humility, fasting both requires and teaches obedience. It is a powerful tool in overcoming disobedience.

Overcoming Strongholds

God used the discipline of fasting to set me free from a stronghold I didn't even know I had. It all started on a perfectly ordinary Sunday in September 1999, when I was sitting in a pew, listening to a sermon. I don't remember the topic or the message, but the preacher started talking about how Dr. Bill Bright from Campus Crusade for Christ had felt the Lord calling him to pray for two million other believers who would fast and pray for forty days for America. The instant I heard that, I *knew* I was one of those two million.

It was beyond a prompting; I was compelled. It was like coming to faith in Jesus as Savior and Lord and just knowing you *must* walk the aisle to the front of the church. Technically, you have a choice, but inwardly, you know there is only one right choice and you must, must, must do it. There was no wavering or second-guessing. I knew in my heart of hearts the Holy Spirit had just called me to fast for forty days.

For two years I had been interceding for our nation and its revival. I had been praying for our leaders in government, our churches, the judiciary, and the military. I was beseeching God for our leaders on the local, state, and national levels. I prayed for every church I happened to drive past. It was a continuing prayer burden. When I heard about Dr. Bright's call to fast for the nation, it was like a light bulb going off over my head. Fasting! Of course!

I had never fasted for more than forty-eight hours before. A forty-day fast had never entered my mind. If not for the crystal clear calling on that Sunday morning, I would never have attempted such a lengthy fast. Really. I had never gone to Bible college or seminary; I was never in full-time ministry or missions. I was a stay-at-home mom with a four-year-old daughter and two-year-old son. I taught Bible studies and led prayer at my local military spouses' ministry.

When I told my husband that I knew I was one of the two million believers who were to fast and pray for America, he didn't even blink. He completely supported me. We went online and downloaded some fasting guidelines from the Campus Crusade Web site. Then I bought a juicer. On Friday I started a three-day fruit and vegetable fast in preparation for the liquids-only fast, and I began the fast the following Monday.

I thought I was fasting and praying for our nation. I was. Yet God used those forty days to transform me. Along with fasting from food, I was led to not read anything but the Bible and other Christian books. I'm a news junkie, and I thought giving up the newspaper and news magazines would be hard. Then one day I caught myself eyeing a *Gourmet* magazine. I so wanted to read it. As I reached for it, I actually ran down a mental checklist: *Did I pray?* Check. *Did I read the Bible?* Check. *Did I journal?* Check. *So now I can do what I want.*

In the middle of a forty-day fast, what did I truly want? Closeness with God? Revival in America? Sadly, no. I wanted to think about food, and not because I was hungry. No, I was *missing* food. I loved food. I had put food in the place of God. Food was my comfort. Food was my joy. Food was my reward. Food was my satisfaction. Food was my consoler. I had an idol. I was stunned. *Idolatry?* As in worshiping something other than the one true God? Me? It was such a harsh word, but it was the truth.

Jesus said, "And you shall know the truth, and the truth shall make you free" (John 8:32 NKJV). I finally understood that verse. Although I had struggled with losing the weight I had gained in pregnancy, I thought it was a question of willpower. I thought I needed more exercise and a better diet. Until the Lord opened my eyes to the truth of my situation, I never saw my weight issue as a spiritual issue. Spiritual problems have spiritual solutions. The spiritual problems of sin, strongholds, and idolatry are never overcome by willpower or force of might or by trying really, really hard. They are overcome by God himself as we submit to Him. God used the discipline of fasting to show me truth and to set me free from my stronghold.

INTERCEDING AND PETITIONING

As I mentioned, I started that forty-day fast thinking it would help me intercede more powerfully for our nation. As I fasted,

I was praying 2 Chronicles 7:14: "If my people, who are called by my name, will humble themselves and pray and seek my face and turn from their wicked ways, then I will hear from heaven, and I will forgive their sin and will heal their land." It all seemed so obvious to me—until I was hit right between the eyes with the truth of my stronghold. Since then, I have learned that all fasting is really about spiritual maturity. Yes, I continued the fast praying for the nation, but God used that fast to transform and mature me.

We may think we're fasting for clarity in knowing God's will, or to intercede, or for strength in the face of spiritual warfare or any other good and holy reason. Here's what really happens: out of His glorious riches, God strengthens us with power, through His Spirit, in our inner being so that Christ dwells in our hearts through faith. We are rooted and established in love. We begin to grasp how wide and long and high and deep is the love of Christ. We begin to know this love and be filled to the measure of all the fullness of God (Ephesians 3:16–19). As you're fasting for another's salvation, or a prodigal's return to Christ, or a marriage proposal, don't be surprised that along with your answered prayer, you are changed for all of eternity.

Fasting for increased power in intercession is a common theme in the Bible. Esther had her maids and all the Jews in Susa fast three days for her before she approached King Xerxes and eventually won deliverance for the Jews (Esther 3–9). The king of Ninevah proclaimed a fast for all of Ninevah to include all the animals, in response to Jonah's message of judgment. The result? "When God saw what they did and how they turned from their evil ways, he relented and did not bring on them the destruction he had threatened" (Jonah 3:10). The Ninevites were not God-fearing. They were a ruthless people. But because they believed the message of the prophet Jonah and fasted, God relented. Whole nations and cities were blessed through fasting and interceding.

This same humbling of self through fasting with prayerful intercession is available to us today. If you have a continuing prayer burden, it might be time to ask God if you can add fasting to your prayers. Fast and pray for those lost family members. Fast and pray for that wayward prodigal. Fast and pray for that failing marriage. Fast and pray for your children as they make important decisions. As you do, yield yourself to His answers and His timing.

Sometimes it's like the old Gospel hymn "Standing in the Need of Prayer":

> It's me, it's me, O Lord,
> standing in the need of prayer;
> Not my mother, not my father . . .
> not my sister, not my brother,
> But it's me, it's me, O Lord,
> standing in the need of prayer.[2]

More than anything, you desire to know what pleases God. You have purposed in your heart to do only what pleases God. You need His help in making a decision. Maybe you're faced with two good choices and need to know which is best. When you've prayed and still are not sure, consider adding fasting to your prayers.

Perhaps you're in a leadership position and you need to know what's best for your group or ministry. When Ezra was permitted by King Artaxerxes to lead the exiled Jews back to Jerusalem, he recognized the danger of the trip and asked God for help:

> There, by the Ahava Canal, I proclaimed a fast, so that we might humble ourselves before God and ask him for a safe

journey for us and our children, with all our possessions. I was ashamed to ask the king for soldiers and horsemen to protect us from enemies on the road, because we had told the king, "The gracious hand of our God is on everyone who looks to him, but his great anger is against all who forsake him." So we fasted and petitioned our God about this, and he answered our prayer. (Ezra 8:21–23)

My friend Sandy and her husband Mark are an army family like we are. One aspect of serving in the army is frequently moving to places you've never been before—with one week, or less, to find and buy a house. It can be nerve-wracking. Sandy shared that she and Mark have fasted and prayed as they seek God's will for where they should live. While they drive around with the Realtor looking at properties and trying to find good houses in good school districts near an army post, they have fasted. They have asked God for guidance and He has not failed them.

SPIRITUAL WARFARE

We are at war. We have always been in spiritual warfare. First, as natural-born citizens of this world, we were enemies of God (Psalm 51:5; Romans 5:10). As enemies of God, we followed Satan and "were by nature deserving of [God's] wrath" (Ephesians 2:3); "As for you, you were dead in your transgressions and sins, in which *you used to live when you followed the ways of this world and of the ruler of the kingdom of the air,* the spirit who is now at work in those who are disobedient" (Ephesians 2:1–2). Then, when we came to saving faith in Jesus, God was no longer our enemy. We were reconciled to God through Jesus (2 Corinthians 5:18). When we trust Jesus, we no longer follow the enemy and live in his kingdom called the world. We cross over into God's kingdom. The war remains; we've just switched sides. Now Satan is our enemy.

Satan, who prowls around like a roaring lion looking for someone to devour (1 Peter 5:8), is described by Jesus as a "murderer from the beginning, not holding to the truth, for there is no truth in him. When he lies, he speaks his native language, for he is a liar and the father of lies" (John 8:44). The Bible also says Satan is our accuser (Revelation 12:10). R. C. Sproul writes in *Pleasing God*, "Satan is not merely our enemy: He is our archenemy."[3] Satan is always against us. He fights dirty, and he will kick us when we're down.

But here is the good news in this war: Jesus won! He "disarmed the powers and authorities, he made a public spectacle of them, triumphing over them by the cross" (Colossians 2:15). Christ's obedience at the cross, His humility, won our victory over the evil one. Satan remains our enemy, but he is a defeated enemy. We don't have to believe his lies about us; we can believe God's truth. We don't have to listen to Satan's accusations; we can believe we are forgiven.

The practice of fasting affects the spiritual warfare in our lives in two ways: it prepares us *for* the warfare and it is a weapon *in* the warfare. In Mark's gospel, we read that the father of a demon-possessed boy brought his son to Jesus' disciples. Although they tried to cast it out, they could not. When Jesus arrives, the father tells Him his whole story—how the boy, since childhood, has been controlled by this violent spirit, how it throws the boy into fire and water and convulses him. Jesus rebukes the spirit and the boy is healed. Later the disciples ask Jesus why they could not cast it out. Jesus responds, "This kind can come out by nothing but prayer and fasting" (Mark 9:29 NKJV). Jesus was not fasting when He cast out the spirit. But early in His ministry He fasted for forty days. He was prepared for the spiritual warfare and was victorious.

Many of us know the verse "Resist the devil, and he will flee from you" (James 4:7) How many of us know that the first sentence in that verse is "Submit yourselves, then, to God"? Before we can resist the devil and have him flee from us, we must first submit ourselves to God. When we're in the middle of warfare and the devil is harassing us, we have the discipline of fasting to bring us to humility and submission before God. Then we can resist the devil and be victorious.

Along with submitting ourselves to God, our other weapon in spiritual warfare is "the sword of the Spirit, which is the word of God" (Ephesians 6:17). Praying God's Word, meditating on it, memorizing it, and speaking it out loud, while fasting, is a most powerful weapon in our arsenal. The Word of God is truth and the perfect antidote to the poison of the enemy's lies.

CALLED TO FAST

Jesus assumed His followers would fast:

> Now John's disciples and the Pharisees were fasting. Some people came and asked Jesus, "How is it that John's disciples and the disciples of the Pharisees are fasting, but yours are not?" Jesus answered, "How can the guests of the bridegroom fast while he is with them? They cannot, so long as they have him with them. But the time will come when the bridegroom will be taken from them, and on that day they will fast." (Mark 2:18–20)

Nowhere does Jesus command fasting. Fasting is not a requirement to be a true disciple. The sole requirement to follow Jesus is faith. Do you believe that Jesus Christ is the way, the truth, and the life? Do you believe that He alone is the way to the Father and eternal salvation? (John 14:6). Are you willing to follow Him?

(Luke 9:23). The disciplines are useful only for building up faith, for equipping the saint to live a life of faith; they have no power to save in themselves.

You might be wondering, *If twenty-four hours is the normal fast, why fast any longer than that?* The Bible is full of examples of longer fasts. Jesus began His public ministry with a forty-day fast.

Then Jesus came from Galilee to the Jordan to be baptized by John. But John tried to deter him, saying, "I need to baptized by you, and do you come to me?" Jesus replied, "Let it be so now, it is proper for us to do this to fulfill all righteousness." Then John consented. As soon as Jesus was baptized, he went up out of the water. At that moment heaven was opened, and he saw the Spirit of God descending like a dove and alighting on him. And a voice from heaven said, "This is my Son, whom I love; with him I am well pleased." *Then Jesus was led by the Spirit* into the wilderness to be tempted by the devil. After fasting forty days and forty nights, he was hungry. (Matthew 3:13–4:2)

Jesus' forty-day fast was not His own idea. He was led by the Spirit, and He obeyed. But we are wise to follow Jesus' example: Fast for more than twenty-four hours only in obedience to a clear call from God.

There are three basic ways you can be called to an extended fast. The first way is a clear call to fast from the Holy Spirit. That was my experience when I joined two million others in fasting for the nation. Usually it's not that dramatic. The second way is best described as a nagging sensation that you should fast. You just can't shake it. At random times, day and night, the idea of a fast keeps popping into your thoughts. (We'll discuss what to do with these thoughts in chapter 4.) The third way to be called to an extended fast is by someone who is in a position of spiritual authority over you. This could be your husband, pastor, or ministry leader.

Many pastors are calling their congregations to fast and pray. One organization called Awakening (*www.awake21.org*) has connected and equipped churches from all over the world to fast and pray for twenty-one days at the start of each New Year. Some pastors are asking their congregations to fast one day a week for the launch of a new ministry or for a particular financial problem facing the church. Liturgical churches have regularly incorporated prayer and fasting during the season of Lent.

The flip side of being called to an extended fast is submitting that call to the spiritual authorities in your life. As strongly as I felt the call to fast and pray for forty days for our nation, it did not overrule the fact that I was called to be a wife and mother first. My husband is my spiritual authority. The Bible is clear on this point (Ephesians 5:22–24; 1 Peter 3:1). It's no good explaining to God why you have to disobey your husband or neglect your children because you believe He's called you to fast. A dear Bible study teacher once described it this way: When you believe your husband is keeping you from doing God's will, obey God by submitting to your husband. Picture yourself ducking to your husband's authority, which puts your husband directly in God's line of sight!

If you are called to fast for more than twenty-four hours, ask the people in spiritual authority over you to pray and confirm this call. Listen to what your Bible study teacher, your pastor, your Sunday school teacher, your parent, or your husband says. If this is God's will, He will certainly make a path for you. Fasting is all about humbling yourself; don't neglect this critical first step.

A Crisis — Asking to Fast

Now that we've established that fasting for more than twenty-four hours should only be as a result of a call from God, here's the exception to that rule: You can ask God about when to fast and if you should fast.

In April 2001 I was overwhelmed. My two-year-old son was scheduled for surgery to have his tonsils and adenoids removed (after thirteen months of recurring infections!), my four-year-old daughter was having extensive dental work, my dad was being examined by an eye specialist for possible macular degeneration, I was preparing to be the speaker for a weekend women's retreat, my husband was traveling overseas, and we had orders to move from Fort Leavenworth, Kansas, to Fort Meade, Maryland, with the obligatory huge yard sale. (In military moves you have to "make weight"—almost everyone has a yard sale before moving.) All of this was happening in the span of four weeks. I hardly knew what to pray for first.

I began a twenty-four-hour fast to ask God if I could fast and pray about everything that was overwhelming me. On April 4 I wrote in my journal, "Thank you, Lord! He let me fast yester-day and He refreshed my soul. He let me hunger for Him and His righteousness and He filled me. And He'll let me fast again next week. So during Holy Week, Sunday to Friday, I will fast and plead, pray, and beseech God Almighty for . . ." and then I listed my prayer concerns. I ended with, "Most of all, I want your heart—to be wholly yours."

I fasted and was able to pray with peace and confidence. Every prayer was answered—my son, daughter, and dad all had great results; I spoke with God's anointing; even the yard sale was a big success and we moved and got quarters at our next duty station. On top of all that, there was one more thing to pray about that I didn't sense until the middle of the fast. During the fast, my husband emailed me to let me know that his travel plans had changed and he would not be home the weekend I was speaking at the women's retreat. I was not happy. I was counting on him to be home to take care of the children. I felt sucker-punched. And mad! After getting all my you've-GOT-to-be-kidding anger out, I finally prayed and God immediately prompted me to ask my mom if she could fly up from Florida for that weekend. She could and she did. The honorarium I received from speaking completely covered her round-trip ticket.

I can honestly say I needed to fast. I needed the power and focus of fasting to survive what I called my "trying month." I have never forgotten that time and how faithfully God met me at each point of need. That fast, although for specific prayer concerns, strengthened my faith as much as it allowed me to pray boldly. I give God all the glory to this very day.

I have not always been permitted to fast when I've asked. One time I remember asking to fast because I felt I was slipping back into bad patterns. I wanted a fresh start and thought a fast would be just the thing. As I was seeking the Lord, He reminded me that He desires obedience, not sacrifice. Slipping into bad patterns was just a whitewashed phrase for disobedience. I didn't need to fast (sacrifice). I needed to repent. Ouch.

A REGULAR PRACTICE

One benefit of fasting is its cumulative nature. I'm convinced that the reason the standard fast in the Bible is twenty-four hours (rather than one long fast each year, for example) is that fasting is best practiced as a regular discipline, a habit. When we consistently humble ourselves and seek God, He is found and we are transformed. Our faith matures, and we discover that we are changed from the inside out.

CHAPTER 3

Should *You* Fast?

Does the Lord delight in burnt offerings and sacrifices as much as in obeying the Lord? To obey is better than sacrifice, and to heed is better than the fat of rams.

—*1 Samuel 15:22*

A biblical fast of liquids only for twenty-four hours is not for everyone. There are sound medical, physical, and psychological reasons not to fast. Physician and author Don Colbert has identified some clear reasons not to fast from food:

You're pregnant

You're nursing

You take medications that must be taken with food

You're diabetic or hypoglycemic

You are being treated for cancer, AIDS, or another serious medical condition

You have congestive heart failure, or your heartbeat skips or is irregular

You've struggled with an eating disorder (anorexia or bulimia)

You take medication for depression or anxiety

You take medication for bipolar disorder, schizophrenia, or another mental illness

Your doctor advises against fasting[1]

Please, please, please don't be foolish about fasting. We are saved by grace through faith (Ephesians 2:8), not by fasting. You are no less a godly woman if you never fast. Godliness and righteousness are by faith, not fasting (Romans 4:3). Use the safeguards of your spiritual authorities to confirm any call to fasting.

If a twenty-four-hour, liquids-only fast won't work for you, it doesn't mean you can't practice fasting. Since fasting is about the wholehearted pursuit of God and the humbling of self, a Daniel-style fast (Daniel 10:3) may be perfect for you. What if you purpose in your heart to fast for twenty-four hours and not eat any meat, snacks, desserts, or wine? During that day you seek God single-mindedly. You spend extra time in the Word.

A non-food fast can also help you focus wholeheartedly on God. A day without TV, radio, iPods, cell phones, Facebook, email, and the Internet, so that you may seek the Lord, is its own kind of fast. Or days without shopping, making absolutely no purchases of any kind (even milk and gas) so you can pursue God, is fasting. When you are fasting, whether it is from food or something else, all the spiritual benefits of a fast are yours.

A final word on non-food fasts: they are just as good, just as holy, as a liquids-only fast. Remember, it's all about grace, not law. It's all about pursuing God with a renewed passion. *How* you pursue God doesn't matter; pursuing God is what matters.

SHOULD CHILDREN FAST?

As fasting has become more widespread, youth groups are hold-ing lock-ins and times of fasting. Some Christian colleges encour-age their students to fast regularly. World Vision sponsors what they call a 30 Hour Famine twice a year where teens raise money and fast to raise awareness for global hunger. Some families fast together for twenty-four hours.

It is generally not recommended that growing children fast. The traditional age to begin fasting is fourteen years old. I believe ex-treme caution should be exercised when involving youth in fasting. Physically, they will probably be fine. However, I have met adults who felt forced to fast as teenagers and resented it. They associate fasting with being denied food, period. The spiritual component, the most important part of fasting, was never realized. Certainly parents can call a fast for the family, but there needs to be genuine spiritual preparation and not just a lock on the kitchen door.

THEN AND NOW

When I completed my first forty-day liquids-only fast, I was in my thirties and I took no prescription medicine (those were the days!). Since then I have been diagnosed with low thyroid function (hypothyroidism) and take a synthetic thyroid medicine every day. One side effect of that medicine is a low vitamin D count and a loss of calcium, so I take a huge vitamin D/calcium pill every day. On top of that, my doctor also prescribes prenatal vitamins. I'm sure those of you who have taken prenatal vitamins are shuddering now. The thyroid medicine must be taken on a completely empty stomach; all the vitamins must be taken with food. The bottom line is, I think the days of forty-day liquids-only fasts are behind me.

I admit I was a little sad when I realized I would probably never have another long liquids-only fast. In the last few years, though, I have been amazed anew at the power of fasting, even with my new constraints. This may sound unbelievable, but fasting for twenty-four hours once every week is as hard and as blessed as a forty-day fast.

When my husband was deployed to Iraq, I learned again that fasting is about the heart, not the type or length of the fast. He was on orders to serve in Iraq three times before he actually deployed. I had always known I would fast and pray for forty days for his safety and for our family when he deployed, but by the time he actually deployed, my hypothyroidism meant I could not do a long liquids-only fast. I remember praying about what to do and immediately sensing that I could still fast and pray for forty days, with a Daniel fast. Having successfully completed several forty-day juice- and water-only fasts, I was pretty confident I could manage a long Daniel fast. But it was so hard! I turned to God as much as during a liquids-only fast: every hamburger called my name, every cookie, every pretzel. I was eating and fasting at the same time and it was remarkably powerful.

Fasting, like any other discipline, isn't static. It varies. Tithing varies with our incomes, serving varies with our commitments, and fasting varies with our health. There may be a season where you don't use the discipline of fasting in your walk with God. And that's perfectly okay.

It Doesn't Hurt to Ask, Part 1

At conferences and retreats, I always teach about the physical and medical limitations to fasting. Just as important, I discuss the spiritual motivations in fasting.

Here, let's start by remembering that God is sovereign, that we can fast and pray about anything, and that God is gracious beyond all understanding. Even so, He does not always give us what we want. A beautiful example of a heartfelt fast that does not result in the hoped-for answer is David's fast recorded in 2 Samuel.

David's adultery with Bathsheba and the subsequent murder of Uriah, her husband, is depicted in 2 Samuel 11:1–25. A few verses later, the story picks up after Bathsheba has mourned her husband's death: "David had her brought to his house, and she became his wife and bore him a son. But the thing David had done displeased the Lord" (2 Samuel 11:27). God sends the prophet Nathan to confront David, but not directly. Instead, Nathan tells David a story of a wealthy man and a poor man from the same village. The wealthy man entertains a guest, but rather than use his vast resources, he takes a lamb from the poor man. And this lamb was not just another farm animal. This lamb was beloved by the poor man and his entire family. Nonetheless, the wealthy man just takes it and kills it for his dinner.

David is enraged by the account and exclaims that the wealthy man deserves to die.

> Then Nathan said to David, "You are the man! This is what the Lord, the God of Israel, says: 'I anointed you king over Israel, and I delivered you from the hand of Saul. I gave your master's house to you, and your master's wives into your arms. I gave you all Israel and Judah. And if all this had been too little, I would have given you even more. Why did you despise the word of the Lord by doing what is evil in his eyes? You struck down Uriah the Hittite with the sword and took his wife to be your own. . . .'"
>
> Then David said to Nathan, "I have sinned against the Lord." Nathan replied, "The Lord has taken away your sin. You are not

going to die. But because by doing this you have shown utter contempt for the Lord, the son born to you will die." (2 Samuel 12:7–9, 13–14)

After Nathan goes home, the Lord strikes the child that Uriah's wife bore to David and the boy becomes ill. David pleads with God for the child.

Of all the things that I might pray for, the life of one of my children is certainly at the top of the list. I would not hesitate to plead with God. But David did not just plead, he fasted. Scripture states, "He fasted and spent the nights lying in sackcloth on the ground" (2 Samuel 12:16). This is a picture of wholehearted pleading, of desperate prayer. David wouldn't even go to bed; he just lay on the ground and fasted. Still, God did not change His mind: "On the seventh day the child died" (2 Samuel 12:18).

"Who Knows?"

Fasting with prayer is powerful and effective. Yet God is God. He is sovereign and just. His will alone prevails. Our sincere fasting and prayer and pleading, for days upon days, won't make God do something other than His will. David's prayers and fasting were fervent, but his prayers and fasting did not change God's judgment.

When David learns his son has died, he doesn't continue fasting or start mourning. Signifying his great faith in God, he does a curious thing. He gets up, washes, and goes to the house of the Lord and worships. Why? Because God is worthy of worship, regardless of our circumstances. Our English word for worship is from the Old English word *weorthscipe*. The root of worship is *worth*. Worship is an intentional recognition of God's worth, even when we don't get what we want. We can only truly worship when we are yielded to God.

Only after David goes to the temple and worships the Lord does he ask his servants for something to eat. Since the custom in David's time was to mourn and fast after a death, and David did the opposite, his servants are bewildered: "Why are you acting this way? While the child was alive, you fasted and wept, but now that the child is dead, you get up and eat!" Look at David's amazing answer: "While the child was still alive, I fasted and wept. I thought, 'Who knows? The Lord may be gracious to me and let the child live'" (2 Samuel 12:21–22).

I love that response! *Who knows? God may yet be gracious.*

Asking God for something, with fasting, is appropriate. It's not bizarre or improper. David asked and fasted, wholeheartedly, in the face of a rebuke and judgment by God's own prophet Nathan. There was nothing ambiguous about Nathan's pronouncement of David's sin, the result of that sin, and the pronouncement that the child would die. And yet David asked. Although the child still died, there was no rebuke given to David because he asked with prayer and fasting. As believers, we may approach God's throne, through faith in Jesus Christ, with all kinds of prayers and petitions. Asking isn't wrong; demanding is. Even when we ask for our heart's highest desire, it must be with yieldedness, a genuine recognition that God alone knows what the best answers to our prayers are.

Until God's judgment was accomplished, David passionately asked God for his heart's desire, the healing of his son. As much as David desired a different outcome from his sin, and fasted and prayed for a different outcome, God's answer remained the same. And David accepted God's good, pleasing, and perfect will (Romans 12:2). David clearly understood what Nathan had said to him and, at the same time, he knew his God was gracious.

David's psalms are full of references to God's graciousness. Our forgiveness is by grace, our salvation is by grace, and God leads us in grace every day.

It Doesn't Hurt to Ask, Part 2

Sometimes God changes His mind. He is moved by the prayers of His people, and He reverses himself. Other times, He doesn't. Since His ways are higher than our ways and His thoughts higher than our thoughts (Isaiah 55:8–9), all we need to do is approach His throne of grace and ask. Our job is to trust Him with the answer and believe that nothing is too difficult for Him (Luke 1:37). Like David, we may know His will, yet ask for His grace.

One of the most stunning examples of answered prayer is King Hezekiah's prayer for healing. It is so amazing that we can read about it in 2 Chronicles 32 and Isaiah 38, as well as this account in 2 Kings 20:1–11:

> In those days Hezekiah became ill and was at the point of death. The prophet Isaiah son of Amoz went to him and said, "This is what the Lord says: Put your house in order, because you are going to die; you will not recover."
>
> Hezekiah turned his face to the wall and prayed to the Lord, "Remember, Lord, how I have walked before you faithfully and with wholehearted devotion and have done what is good in your eyes." And Hezekiah wept bitterly.
>
> Before Isaiah had left the middle court, the word of the Lord came to him: "Go back and tell Hezekiah, the ruler of my people, 'This is what the Lord, the God of your father David, says: I have heard your prayer and seen your tears; I will heal you. On the third day from now you will go up to the temple of the Lord. I will add fifteen years to your life. And

I will deliver you and this city from the hand of the king of Assyria. I will defend this city for my sake and for the sake of my servant David.' "

Then Isaiah said, "Prepare a poultice of figs." They did so and applied it to the boil, and he recovered.

Hezekiah had asked Isaiah, "What will be the sign that the Lord will heal me and that I will go up to the temple of the Lord on the third day from now?" Isaiah answered, "This is the Lord's sign to you that the Lord will do what he has promised: Shall the shadow go forward ten steps, or shall it go back ten steps?" "It is a simple matter for the shadow to go forward ten steps," said Hezekiah. "Rather, have it go back ten steps."

Then the prophet Isaiah called upon the Lord, and the Lord made the shadow go back the ten steps it had gone down on the stairway of Ahaz.

Wow. Not just healing but minutes added to the day! Plus, the defeat of the Assyrian enemy!

I am struck by Hezekiah's prayer and his request for a sign. Hezekiah's entire prayer was only one sentence long. He didn't argue with God or ask if Isaiah had somehow gotten the message wrong. He didn't plead for God to spare him because of his responsibilities as commander of Israel's armies. No, he just asked God to remember his faithfulness, his devotion to God, and his righteousness. Then, when Isaiah immediately returns with the good news—healing! and fifteen more years of life!—Hezekiah asks for a sign. Really?

Yet God is not offended. He even lets Hezekiah pick the sign. Should the shadow go forward or backward? *Very well, back ten steps.* And so it happens. If this is not an encouragement to ask, to pray boldly, to *believe* God, I don't know what is.

Gideon, like Hezekiah, famously asked for a sign from God (Judges 6–8). Today we might use the word *confirmation*.

Does asking for a sign, a confirmation, show a lack of faith? Scripture says no. Both Gideon and Hezekiah received their signs, Gideon repeatedly. The real question is the heart. Is your heart fully prepared to do whatever God has asked you to do (believe in recovery from illness; defeat a huge enemy army) and you just want to make sure you know exactly what God's will is? Or are you testing God (prove that you are God before I will believe)?

With right motives, it never hurts to ask.

In *Fasting Can Change Your Life,* Elmer Towns shares a wonderful story about fasting and healing from cancer. The dean of students at Liberty University, Vernon Brewer, had been diagnosed with cancer. Loved by the students and faculty, his prognosis of having just a short time to live hit the university community hard. Jerry Falwell, president of the university at the time, designated a day in April to fast and pray for Brewer. Five thousand people fasted and prayed for twenty-four hours. Towns writes, "I wish I could say that God healed Vernon Brewer instantly, but it did not happen that way. . . . So while the healing was not instantaneous—it took over a year—nevertheless, it was miraculous. They predicted he would live for only another three to six months, but, obviously, the prediction was wrong because I see him alive all the time."[2]

God answers prayer.

What desperate prayer do you have? Where can God show His graciousness to you? I pray that your prayer is answered with more graciousness than you can ever ask for. I pray that like Hezekiah, your prayer would be answered immediately and you would have a sure confirmation. And I pray that like David, you will trust God's graciousness to be the best and most loving answer, especially when it is not what you prayed for.

THE INTERSECTION OF GRACE, SACRIFICE, AND WORSHIP

Accepting God's will when it is the exact opposite of what we want is a tremendous act of worship. Grace lets us ask, and ask with all of our heart. Yieldedness lets us worship when the answer is no. Worship is the faith-filled recognition of God's worth, His holiness, and His sovereignty, with a rock-solid belief that God loves us, regardless of our circumstances. I can't think of anything more difficult in our faith walk than believing God and worshiping Him when our hearts are broken.

This yieldedness is a sacrifice. It is a higher sacrifice than fasting. It is obedience, which God desires more than any fleshly sacrifice (1 Samuel 15:22). God is after our heart's surrender, the sacrifice of self to Him, not a mere fleshly sacrifice. Fasting is a powerful tool in helping us get to this yielded position.

Worship, true worship, requires this kind of sacrifice. Larry Crabb captures this concept in his book *The PAPA Prayer.* He writes:

> For most of my adult life, the notion that worship at its core is sacrifice never took hold. I'm not sure I ever heard it. I went along with my church culture, which seemed to think worship was about feeling emotional about God, especially when He behaved properly, which meant that He did what we asked Him to do. Then we shared our appreciation in musical and sentence prayers when we felt better.[3]

Both David and Hannah worshiped with sacrifice. Scripture tells us that early the next morning, the day after Hannah had poured out her soul to the Lord, she worshiped the Lord. She worshiped Him not knowing He would give her Samuel and his five brothers and sisters. She worshiped Him because He is worthy of worship, regardless of His answer to her fasting prayer. David worshiped the Lord when he learned that God did not spare his son. He did not even end his fast and eat until he had gone to the house of the Lord to worship. They both understood that the fasting wasn't the sacrifice; the yieldedness to God's will was the sacrifice.

Prayer and fasting, with good motives, is a blessed gift for every believer. We have been given the right, through the blood of Jesus Christ, to approach God Almighty and ask, petition, and plead. Then, in faith, we yield and trust that His answer is best. The guarantee of asking is not that we will instantly gain our heart's desire; the guarantee is that we will touch the heart of God and He will do *whatever* is best for us.

I often think of Jesus' mother at His arrest, trial, and sentencing. Certainly Mary would have been praying—maybe with tears, maybe with fasting. As a mother, my guess is that each of her mother's prayers was unanswered: Jesus was not released by Pontius Pilate, He was beaten horribly, nailed to a cross, and died. And yet without His perfect sacrifice—obeying His Father's will right through a painful death—there would be no hope and no salvation for the entire world.

It Is Better to Obey Than to Sacrifice

For us, the sacrifice of fasting won't make up for disobedience. Fasting can accompany repentance, but fasting does not accomplish the repentance. Fasting can accompany a rededication, a new desire to follow the Lord, but it's the daily walking out of the rededication that brings our souls closer to God. Even a long fast means nothing apart from a heart willing to yield and obey.

One of the most important lessons the Old Testament teaches us is that rote sacrifice, without obedience, is idolatry. In 1 Samuel,

Samuel tells King Saul that he is to accomplish God's judgment and destroy the Amalekites. Saul conquers them, but instead of killing everything, he saves the best sheep, cattle, and lambs to sacrifice to the Lord. Samuel confronts Saul:

> Samuel said, "Although you were once small in your own eyes, did you not become the head of the tribes of Israel? The Lord anointed you king over Israel. And he sent you on a mission, saying, 'Go and completely destroy those wicked people, the Amalekites; wage war against them until you have wiped them out.' Why did you not obey the Lord? Why did you pounce on the plunder and do evil in the eyes of the Lord?"
>
> "But I did obey the Lord," Saul said. "I went on the mission the Lord assigned me. I completely destroyed the Amalekites and brought back Agag their king. The soldiers took sheep and cattle from the plunder, the best of what was devoted to God, in order to sacrifice them to the Lord your God at Gilgal." (15:17–21)

No remorse, no confession. Saul is so busy justifying himself that he doesn't seem to understand the seriousness of his disobedience. I don't judge Saul too harshly, though—too many times I want to explain to God that, although His idea is great, mine must be better. *Really, Lord, can't you see it my way?*

> But Samuel replied: "Does the Lord delight in burnt offerings and sacrifices as much as in obeying the Lord? To obey is better than sacrifice, and to heed is better than the fat of rams. For rebellion is like the sin of divination, and arrogance like the evil of idolatry. Because you have rejected the word of the Lord, he has rejected you as king." (15:22–23)

Real obedience is motivated by love for God. God desires our responsive love; there is no sacrifice, nothing we can give Him or do for Him that pleases Him more than our willingness to believe

Him and obey. Oswald Chambers describes this eloquently in his classic *My Utmost for His Highest:*

> The counterfeit of obedience is a state of mind in which you create your own opportunities to sacrifice yourself, and your zeal and enthusiasm are mistaken for discernment. It is easier to sacrifice yourself than to fulfill your spiritual destiny which is stated in Romans 12:1–2. [Therefore, I urge you, brothers, in view of God's mercy, to offer your bodies as living sacrifices, holy and pleasing to God—this is your spiritual act of worship. Do not conform any longer to the pattern of this world, but be transformed by the renewing of your mind. Then you will be able to test and approve what God's will is—his good, pleasing and perfect will.] *It is much better to fulfill the purpose of God in your life by discerning His will than it is to perform great acts of self-sacrifice. "Behold, to obey is better than sacrifice . . ."*[4]

INSINCERE FASTING IS NO FASTING AT ALL

Fasting with the wrong motives is its own kind of disobedience. When we know what delights God, when we have a call to obey God in some matter, there are no substitutions allowed. We can't choose a twenty-four-hour fast instead of giving, or a fast instead of offering hospitality.

During the Israelites' exile from Israel and Jerusalem, they set up a fasting schedule to mourn the destruction of the temple and Jerusalem. After nearly seventy years of fasting in exile, certain leaders approached the prophet Zechariah. They asked if they should continue this fasting practice. The Lord Almighty responds to their question though Zechariah: "When you fasted and mourned in the fifth and seventh months for the past seventy years, *was it really for me that you fasted?*" (Zechariah 7:5).

On the outside, fasting can look so spiritual, so righteous. God doesn't look at the outside; He looks at the heart (1 Samuel 16:7). Fasting will not fool God. I, we, must remember that obedience, that is, loving God and loving others, is the real reason to fast (or to practice any of the disciplines). God's call for the Israelites was clear:

> And the word of the Lord came again to Zechariah: "This is what the Lord Almighty said: 'Administer true justice; show mercy and compassion to one another. Do not oppress the widow or the fatherless, the foreigner or the poor. Do not plot evil against each other'" (Zechariah 7:8–10).

The Israelites did the very opposite of what God had called them to do through His prophets. They did not administer justice; they were not merciful and compassionate. But they did oppress widows, orphans, aliens, and the poor. Worse yet, their thoughts were evil. This sin resulted in their exile.

> But they refused to pay attention; stubbornly they turned their backs and covered their ears. They made their hearts as hard as flint and would not listen to the law or to the words that the Lord Almighty had sent by his Spirit through the earlier prophets. So the Lord Almighty was very angry.
>
> "When I called, they did not listen; so when they called, I would not listen," says the Lord Almighty. "I scattered them with a whirlwind among all the nations, where they were strangers. The land they left behind them was so desolate that no one traveled through it. This is how they made the pleasant land desolate" (Zechariah 7:11–14).

Scripture reveals that God was fully aware of the Israelites' fasting schedule. However, His desire was not only for the restoration of the temple but for the restoration of Israel's relationship to Him. He longed for their hearts; He longed for their genuine love of Him, for genuine love for each other. Instead, He got fasting.

FASTING IS NOT A TRANSACTION

I'm guessing you have had the opportunity to baby-sit at some point in your life. And I'll guess a child or two was a handful, bless their hearts. Perhaps you encountered a very determined, very loud four-year-old who told you "You're NOT the boss of me!" in response to your perfectly reasonable, "You have to put your shoes on to go to the playground." No matter how much yelling, sulking, or crying that preschooler does, the rule is still no shoes, no playground. You are not mean or unreasonable; you just know what's best. You, unlike the four-year-old, are fully aware of the dangers and hazards at a public playground—broken glass and dog poop, for starters.

Sometimes when we ask God for something and He says no, we act a lot like that four-year-old. We beg. We plead. We nag. Still, God is not moved to our way of thinking. We know we can ask Him for anything, with or without fasting (John 14:14, Matthew 7:7). Jesus also plainly tells us, "But when you fast, put oil on your head and wash your face, so that it will not be obvious to others that you are fasting, but only to your Father, who is unseen; *and your Father, who sees what is done in secret, will reward you*" (Matthew 6:17–18). Fasting is rewarded.

Maybe we think if we just add some fasting to our prayers, we could make God answer our prayers . . . our way.

Here's the danger with focusing on the rewards of fasting: We can easily slip into a mindset that God *must* answer our fasting prayers. In other words, we start thinking that we have earned our prayer requests through the good work of fasting. Nothing could be further from the truth. Fasting is not a reward system. As Pastor John Piper writes, this thinking "would dishonor God by turning his free grace into a business transaction. It would imply that fasting springs ultimately from our own will, and that this self-created discipline is then offered to God for recompense. This is a great dishonor to God because it claims for us what belongs only to God, namely, the ultimate initiative of prayer and fasting. In this way we put ourselves in the place of God and nullify the freedom of his grace."[5]

There are plenty of bad reasons to fast: against sound medical advice, as a sacrifice instead of obedience, or even insincere, ritualistic fasting. But the worst kind of fasting is a fast that reduces an amazing spiritual discipline to a business transaction that strips away all grace. I am praying that none of us, myself included, will ever be tempted to do that. Instead, let's choose to fast humbly and obediently, and wait with great hope for God's graceful answers to our prayers.

CHAPTER 4

Getting Ready to Fast

In their hearts humans plan their course, but the Lord establishes their steps.

—Proverbs 16:9

It's exciting when you feel the stirring of the Spirit and realize you are being called to fast. If you're like me, you might feel a little nervous and expectant all at once. You also might be thinking, *Now what?* The answer to that question is preparation.

Good preparation is the key to fasting success. The opposite is also true: Poor preparation can easily lead to failure (which I discuss in chapter 7). Since fasting is physical and spiritual all at the same time, the preparation is equally physical and spiritual. The amount and kind of preparation corresponds to the length of the fast.

HEARING THE CALL TO FAST

The starting point in spiritual preparation for fasting is to be still and listen to God. Each of us hears our Lord's voice. He speaks to us in four main ways: through His Word, through the Spirit in prayer, through the church and other believers, and through circumstances. God speaks to His children. Why? Over and over in the Bible, God speaks to reveal himself (Father, Son, and Holy Spirit) and to reveal His will. How many times in the Old Testament do we read ". . . and they will know I am the Lord"? From Abraham to Moses and Pharaoh to the later prophets, God is revealing himself, His authority, and His salvation. He desires that all would come to a saving knowledge of Him through Jesus Christ, and He reveals His will through the created world, the heavens, and in man's hearts (Romans 1:19–20).

If God reveals His will to the lost of this world, how much more will He reveal His will concerning you, His beloved daughter?

If you are being called to fast, you will know it. You will hear the Lord's voice: "Whether you turn to the right or to the left, your ears will hear a voice behind you, saying 'This is the way; walk in it'" (Isaiah 30:21). Sometimes I liken it to a gentle nagging—as I'm going through my day I can't seem to get the idea of a fast out of my mind. Then I sit quietly and ask God if He is calling me to fast. Usually the answer comes in His Word, sometimes in a sermon or in prayer.

Ask God outright: Am I being called to fast? If so, for how long? And what kind of a fast? Partial or liquids only? When we seek God with all our heart, He answers: "This is what the Lord says, he who made the earth, the Lord who formed it and established it—the Lord is his name: 'Call to me and I will answer you and tell you great and unsearchable things you do not know'" (Jeremiah 33:2–3). As you pray about a fast, believe that as you call to the Lord, He will answer you and tell you what you need to know. Most often He will answer you in His Word. If you're not sure you are being called to fast, wait. Sometimes, like my first forty-day fast, the call to fast was crystal clear. Often, I just have a sense I should fast; I start praying and asking God if He is calling me to fast. Then, in my regular quiet time, I hear the answer. God desires for us to know His will and do it.

The bottom line is it's like your salvation experience; you will know.

The key to preparing for a fast is to remember that it is God-initiated. Pastor Mark Buchanan in his book *Your God Is Too Safe* expertly describes this truth:

> Fasting is a God-led, Spirit-driven activity. It is not just your own idea. It is not a legalistic requirement. It is not a work we perform. It is not a weight-loss technique. It is not a hunger strike. No, it is a God and Spirit work, a response to the leading and the driving of the Godhead. In fact, fasting begins with a hunger for more of God's direction in your life. Fasting is born of an appetite for more of God's presence, wanting God to lead, wanting the Spirit to drive. And what He often leads us and drives us into is a fast.[1]

A FASTING PLAN

Once I'm sure I am responding to God's invitation to fast, I ask Him how long He would have me fast. As I wrote earlier, a twenty-four-hour fast is a great discipline to add to your faith walk. Anything longer should be as a result of a call from God. He initiates our fasting, we respond in faith. In your regular Bible reading, you are going to be amazed at the amount of number references. You will come across words such as:

One day

Several days

Three

Seven

Nine

Ten

Fourteen

Twenty-one

Forty

Whether I know the length of the fast or I'm not yet sure how long to fast, I get my calendar and start praying. I sit with my calendar in my lap and ask God to show me the start day and the end day. Once again, you will be amazed at how often there is an unscheduled chunk of time on your calendar that perfectly matches the length of the fast you are called to do.

I also pray to know if the fast is a liquids-only or partial fast. A liquids-only fast for more than twenty-four hours involves preparation and scheduled rest time during the fast. Sometimes when I'm praying over my calendar, I can see I have social commitments that will make a liquids-only fast very difficult. That may be all the confirmation I need to do a partial fast. If I'm still not sure, I keep praying. I wait. I look at my calendar and see if I can reschedule any commitments. What I don't do is assume I must fast a certain way at a certain time. If God is calling me to fast and pray about something, He'll make it clear to me (John 10:1–5).

When you are confident of God's call for you to fast, write down your fasting plan. It can be an informal note on your calendar or a more formal plan. You'll want to include the spiritual reason you believe God is calling you to fast and any Scripture that goes with that reason or call. You'll certainly want to write down the length of the fast (one meal to forty days) and the type of the fast. If it's a partial fast, what is included? What isn't included? You might want to use a model something like this:

God is calling me to fast and pray for _____.
The fast is water only/water and juices/a Daniel fast/a partial fast: _____.
If it's a partial fast, the foods I am not eating are _____ and the foods I am eating are _____.
The fast starts _____ and ends _____.
My Scripture verse is _____.
My prayer partner(s) is _____.

Writing down a plan is one of the most important things you can do when you are preparing to fast. It is quite common that once the fast begins, and you're hungry, you might start to doubt your call to fast. Thoughts like, *Is this really for a full twenty-four hours? Not just for one meal?* may come into your mind. When you have a written plan, you can assure yourself that you did indeed hear the Lord and are doing His will. When I am in a Daniel fast (either no sweets, meats, or treats, or a fruits- and vegetables-only fast), I have found it absolutely essential to write down what is and is not permissible.

A TIME TO FEAST AND A TIME TO FAST

As I am looking for the right time to fast, I take into consideration the social activities I have. I do not ever, ever recommend fasting during the holidays. There is a time for feasting and a time for fasting. I once taught a workshop on fasting at a women's conference in early November. The following day, one of the ladies in the class came to me and said she was being called to fast and pray for forty days. (Her husband's unit was getting ready to deploy to war.) She believed she was to start the fast right away. I affirmed the power of fasting and praying for her husband and his unit, but I did everything in my power to dissuade her from starting the fast at that time. I reminded her that Thanksgiving was coming up. She would also need time for the important physical and spiritual preparation necessary with such a long fast. I pleaded with her to wait. However, she was convinced that she was called and started the fast anyway. Within two weeks she had broken the fast and was greatly discouraged. I believe she heard God's call but missed His timing.

I also avoid birthdays. In our home, the birthday boy or girl (kids and grown-ups) gets to pick the dinner meal (even if it's McDonald's!) and the type of cake. It is a feasting time, a time of celebration. I avoid the first week of school, too. I need all the energy I can get when I'm getting back into the early morning school routine. Since we're a military family, we move often (eighteen homes in twenty-seven years so far). I never fast during a move. Moving is too physically and mentally exhausting. Graduations, weddings, and other times of celebration are also not the best times to fast.

Whether planning for a one-meal fast or for several days, use the commonsense wisdom God has given you. If your periods really knock you out, avoid fasting at that time of the month. If you have a deadline or big project at work, take that into consideration. I know a man who had a physically demanding job who was called to a liquids-only fast. For him, liquids included all kinds of soups so he would have the energy he needed for his work. When I was fasting for forty days the first time, I was teaching undergraduate classes on a compressed schedule. I lectured for nearly three hours four nights a week, plus the preparation. I was juicing carrots and apples three times a day—a huge amount of nutrition for a liquids-only fast. It was exactly what I needed.

FASTING ON GOD'S TIMETABLE

As much as "there is a time for everything, and a season for every activity under the heavens" (Ecclesiastes 3:1), it is God alone who knows those times. Practical considerations fall before God's timing for us to fast. In one season I was called to fast right when school was starting. It was August 2001, and I had a very clear call to fast for thirty days. It was a bit unusual, though, because I had no big, obvious reason. I wrote in my journal that I was fasting for personal holiness and victory, for the military ministry I serve in, and for my mother-in-law, who had just moved to Florida. I did not have a verse to pray throughout the fast. Yet the call to fast was so strong, I knew I had to obey.

The twelfth day of that fast was Tuesday, September 11, 2001. In my early-morning quiet time, the verses that leaped off of the page for me were from 2 Corinthians 10:3–6: "For though we live in the world, we do not wage war as the world does. The weapons we fight with are not the weapons of the world. On the contrary, they have divine power to demolish strongholds. We demolish arguments and every pretension that sets itself up against the knowledge of God, and we take captive every thought to make it obedient to Christ. And we will be ready to punish every act of disobedience, once your obedience is complete."

By 9:40 that morning, I knew exactly why I was fasting.

My husband, John, was assigned to the army headquarters at the Pentagon. He had an important briefing to give to his two-star general that morning. I was praying for him and the briefing all morning. When the first plane hit the World Trade Center, my sweet neighbor, Rosie, came over and told me. I didn't turn on the TV, though. I just kept praying. When the plane hit the Pentagon, Rosie came running back over. This time I turned on the TV and was stunned. I tried to call John. No answer at his desk or on his cell phone. I left messages on both phones and kept trying to reach him. I knew John would call if he could. About fifteen minutes later Rosie came by and asked if I had heard from John. Not yet. Half an hour later, she asked again. Still nothing.

Then she stopped coming over to ask. She—and I—realized I might not hear from John again. As I sat watching the smoke pour out of the Pentagon, thoughts swirled in my mind: If John was dead, would I have to tell his mother? And where are those life insurance policies? And why hasn't he called?! As I was trying to pray, the Spirit reminded me of a Bible study. In *Experiencing God,* Henry Blackaby wrote that whenever you find yourself in difficult circumstances, look at your situation with the cross of Christ in the foreground and your problem in the background. God's love for us was forever settled at the cross. I focused on that truth and prayed, "Heavenly Father, I know you love me. That was settled at the cross. I want John to be okay. I know that you alone know what is best for me. I don't want to be a widow, but I am not going to argue with you over what is best for me."

An immediate sense of peace washed over me. Whatever happened, God had me in His hand.

The plane had hit right underneath John's office. The jet-fueled fireball would certainly have killed them all but for the brand-new renovations on that wedge of the Pentagon. The fire was so hot that the computer towers melted to the floor. Every single person in his office made it out alive. John was in the corridor when the plane hit. It knocked him off of his feet. A civilian secretary was also knocked down and remained curled up on the floor, very shaken. John pulled her up and said, "Ma'am, we need to get out of here." It's my favorite part of our testimony—always the officer and a gentleman, he says "ma'am" in the middle of an explosion! He was able to escort her through the closing fire doors, and they got out of the burning Pentagon.

Outside, he met up with other people from the office. One man had a cell phone with a signal. He called his wife and then passed the phone to over forty people. Each one gave her his or her name and home phone number, and that dear woman called every single number.

At 11:09 a.m. I got a phone call from a complete stranger, saying, "I have a message for you: John Nelson is okay." It was the best phone call I ever got.

THE SPIRIT INTERCEDES

> In the same way, the Spirit helps us in our weakness. We do not know what we ought to pray for, but the Spirit himself intercedes for us through wordless groans. And he who searches our hearts knows the mind of the Spirit, because the Spirit intercedes for God's people in accordance with the will of God. (Romans 8:26–27)

I believe all those fasting prayers for John about the briefing were taken by the Holy Spirit and refashioned into prayers for John's safety, in accordance with God's will. In her book *The Power of a Praying Nation*, Stormie Omartian writes that she was awakened at 3:30 on September 11 with an overwhelming sense of dread. She prayed for her family members and friends and everyone she could think of and then finally went back to sleep. When she awoke, the planes had hit.[2] I believe God used her prayers, and the prayers of countless other saints, on that awful day.

In the days that followed, as horrible as the tragedy of lost life was, there was story after story of people who were spared. The Twin Towers were not full that morning; many people had not yet arrived for the workday. The plane had hit the Pentagon in the *one* wedge that had been completely renovated with blast-proof windows and reinforced walls. Even in the midst of this evil, there was God's mercy.

As much as I believe there are practical things to consider when praying about a fast, when you're called to fast, fast. If it's during an inconvenient time, ask God for clear confirmation. He will make His will known to you. Then obey.

Preparing Physically for a Fast

The physical preparations for a fast depend on the length and type of the fast. A partial fast, such as a Daniel fast, or fasting from a certain food or food group, does not require the physical preparation that a liquids-only fast requires. A one-meal or twenty-four-hour fast has minimal physical requirements, while a forty-day fast has several important preparation requirements.

Twenty-Four-Hour, Liquids-Only Fasts

Since there is minimal physical preparation for a twenty-four-hour fast, the risk is forgetting that fasting isn't just not eating. Again, simply skipping breakfast and lunch is not fasting; it's just not eating. So make sure your twenty-four-hour fast is preceded by good spiritual preparation.

The best physical preparation for a twenty-four-hour fast is to increase your liquid intake the day before and to eat a normal or smaller meal before you start the fast. Don't eat a feast and then immediately start fasting. The food will sit in your stomach like a rock; you will be very uncomfortable and you may be nauseous and throw up. For the same reason, it is best to avoid heavy, greasy, or fried foods before any fasting.

I am currently fasting for twenty-four hours once a week. I usually fast on Tuesday, which means the fast begins on Monday evening and ends on Tuesday evening. I plan a simple dinner on Monday night. Maybe baked chicken, broccoli, rice, and salad, or spaghetti and meatballs (and I skip the meatballs) with salad, or soup and salad. I don't make pot roast and gravy, bacon and eggs (we love breakfast foods for supper), pork chops, or anything too rich and heavy.

Two- to Three-Day Fasts

The preparation for a fast lasting up to seventy-two hours is the same as a twenty-four-hour fast. If you are ready and called to fast longer than twenty-four hours, a thirty-six-hour fast and, my favorite, a forty-hour fast, are powerful and effective.

Four- to Seven-Day Fasts

Once you start fasting for more than three days, and as you approach seven days, your digestive system will start to rest. The physical preparation becomes critical. Everything from the preparation for a twenty-four-hour fast applies and more.

The day before I start a fast that will last up to seven days, I not only increase my liquid intake, I avoid ALL fats. If I eat protein, it is very lean or low-fat/nonfat dairy. I do not eat any meat. I eat primarily grains, fruits, and vegetables. I might eat whole-wheat toast with jam or raisin bran with skim milk, or low-fat yogurt for breakfast. The rest of the day I will eat fruits and vegetables. I often include lentil soup, pea soup, and tomato soup. For grains, I like brown rice and oatmeal. Eating foods with high fiber content will keep you from any constipation issues (which are rare because of all the fluids you drink). If you're a coffee drinker, you will find it helpful to start reducing your caffeine intake if you're going to stop drinking coffee during the fast.

Eight- to Twenty-One-Day Fasts

Preparation is critical for a liquids-only fast that will last more than one week and up to three weeks. Follow the same guidelines as for a four- to seven-day fast, but do so for *at least* two days prior to the fast, *and* eat less. The point of this physical preparation is to prepare your body for the complete cessation of food for a long time.

Thirty- and Forty-Day Fasts

If you are called to a longer fast, more than twenty-one days and up to forty days, you must take time to prepare: AT LEAST three days of preparation under the guidelines above. I started preparing for my first forty-day fast on a Friday. I had three meals of fruits and vegetables that day. On Saturday, I had two meals (lunch and dinner) of fruits and vegetables. On Sunday I had one meal (lunch) of vegetables. I remember it was cooked squash. Although I had never fasted for more than forty-eight hours before this forty-day fast, I was physically prepared and had absolutely no problems throughout the fast.

What Kind of Liquids?

The types of liquids I drink also vary with the length of the fast. As I mentioned in chapter 1, if it's a twenty-four-hour fast, almost any liquid will work. The same is true for up to seventy-two hours. Well, maybe not milk shakes or frozen Frappuccinos!

When you're fasting for more than three days, you want to avoid any liquid with protein because protein kicks your digestive system out of rest (and back into hunger). Fruit and vegetable juices, lots of water, vegetable broth, even all-fruit smoothies are great when you're fasting. The natural sugar and good taste of the juice strengthens you and helps you keep on the fast. When I was fasting for forty days the first time, I used a juicer and juiced a mixture of carrots and apples at least twice a day. If you don't have a juicer, you don't need to run out and buy one. There are plenty of fresh fruit juices and juice blends available in the grocery store. I like the Odwalla and Naked brands. Just be careful to read the label; you want to make sure the grams of protein are zero and that the ingredients are just fruits and/ or vegetables.

Over the years I have learned which juices work best for me, just as you will. Many people recommend avoiding acidic juices like orange juice and tomato juice. I can't tolerate orange juice when I'm not fasting, so I certainly avoid it when I'm fasting. However, tomato juice is a complete blessing to me when I fast. Also, V8 juice (low-sodium) and V8 juice blends are great. On the other hand, apple juice, which is highly recommended in fasting, gives me diarrhea every time. Needless to say, I avoid that one.

I also drink vegetarian vegetable broth, Campbell's tomato soup (no protein, just tomatoes and water), Canada Dry's green tea ginger ale, Ocean Spray's Cran-Energy cranberry juice, Lipton green tea with citrus, and all the cranberry blend juices, any brand. I look for the highest amount of fruit with the least amount of sugar. My go-to drink is one-third cranberry juice and two-thirds seltzer water in a large cup. I also like hot water with a wedge of lemon, and sometimes a little sugar or honey. On longer fasts (more than three days), I learned how important electrolytes are.

I drink sports drinks, such as Gatorade, PowerAde, and Propel. I have found Glacéau's Vitamin Water to be helpful, too.

PREPARING SPIRITUALLY FOR A FAST

After you have heard the call to fast, the next step is to ask God why you're fasting. Often this is clear at the time of the call. But sometimes it's not answered until you are in the fast itself. I always ask God to show me why He is calling me to fast and why now. I can't tell you how many times I ask this question, get an answer, and then, in the middle of the fast, a whole additional reason for the fast is revealed. It's almost like you need to be in that fasting, submitted-heart place in your soul before God can share with you what He's really after.

At the same time, like the start of my 9/11 fast, you may not get a clear answer for why this fast and why now. That is not an impediment to fasting. Trust that God will show you the answers in His perfect timing. It may be during or even after the fast.

Confessing Sin

Not surprisingly, part of being still and hearing God call you to fast is self-examination. I like to start by praying Psalm 139: 23–24: "Search me, God, and know my heart; test me and know my anxious thoughts. See if there is any offensive way in me, and lead me in the way everlasting." I wait and see if the Spirit brings any unconfessed sin to mind. Don't go rooting around in your past looking for sin. God is perfect; if there's something you need to confess and repent, He'll lovingly show you.

Next to being called to fast, confessing sin is an absolutely vital step. I try to do this daily, and I especially do this before I fast. Don't be surprised when, sometime in your fast, some sin comes to mind for you to confess. After years of fasting, I pretty much expect to have some past sin revealed. And, yes, that's after I've confessed all my known sin while I am preparing to fast.

I was fasting in the fall of 2000, driving in the car on an errand, when a complete tableau crossed my mind. In 1990, *ten years prior,* my husband was a graduate student at Virginia Tech. I was going to meet him on campus. There was a small parking lot right behind his building. As usual, it was full. As I circled around, I spied a car pulling out of a spot. I pulled over and put my blinker on. Suddenly, another car came from the other direction and slipped into *my* spot. Oh, was I steamed. I thought the guy was a jerk. Since there were no other spots, I drove on to another, farther, parking area and forgot about the incident.

Here's the rest of the story. That first parking area required a permit, which I did not have. The car that stole my space had that permit. When the whole scene flashed before my mind ten years later, seemingly from out of nowhere, the Lord opened my eyes: I was the jerk in that scenario. I was bitter and unforgiving against some poor guy who actually was authorized to park there. Tears sprang to my eyes. I immediately confessed my rotten behavior and worse attitude.

Somehow the discipline of fasting puts me in a tender, humble state and I can receive correction and rebuke with joy. I want to be righteous more than I want to be right. God uses fasting to prune me; He "cuts off every branch in me that bears no fruit, while every branch that does bear fruit he prunes so that it will be even more fruitful" (John 15:2). Fasting is the Master Gardener's effective tool. And notice when this pruning occurred. Not in my quiet time, not during praise and worship (although that's another good time for my eyes to be opened), not during any spiritual activity. I was just driving along in the middle of a fast and the Spirit used my idle mind to reveal some dead wood in my soul.

I want to emphasize that the spiritual preparation for fasting is important, but I also want you to know that as much as you prepare, as deeply as you let the Spirit examine you prior to fasting, it is very common for something to be revealed while you're fasting.

Whether you discover your need to confess a sin or to forgive someone before, during, or even after the fast, here are some insights about practicing forgiveness.

Forgiving Others

When we've been wronged or we feel like we've been wronged (like my parking spot incident) or hurt, our first desire is often vengeance. We want the offender to get what she or he deserves! Somewhere in our souls the Spirit is whispering "forgive, forgive," but it's hard to hear His voice over our own demands for payback. The truth is, forgiveness isn't natural; it's supernatural. Forgiveness is the work of the Spirit.

In the New Testament there are several verses exhorting Christians to forgive others, including:

> For if you forgive other people when they sin against you, your heavenly Father will also forgive you. But if you do not forgive others their sins, your Father will not forgive your sins. (Matthew 6:14–15)

> And when you stand praying, if you hold anything against anyone, forgive them, so that your Father in heaven may forgive you your sins. (Mark 11:25)

> Forgive, and you will be forgiven. (Luke 6:37)

We must forgive. It is a command. And on top of that, if we do not forgive others for their sins, our Father will not forgive our sins. We are forgiven in proportion to the way we forgive others. Please don't panic. This is about forgiving others, not your salvation. In Christ, you are forgiven, and His blood is sufficient to cover every sin you have committed or will commit, including the sin of unforgiveness. This is about your walk of faith, the amount of grace in your life. Our growth, our spiritual maturity, requires our obedience. When we disobey (refuse to forgive), we thwart the Spirit's work in our lives. He will convict us at every opportunity and relentlessly pursue us to return to our Lord. Yet we have a will and we can choose to obey or disobey.

When we recognize our true position as sinners saved by grace, it is much easier for us to submit ourselves to the Holy Spirit's work of forgiveness. Our proper understanding of the forgiveness purchased for us in Jesus Christ is the starting point for all forgiveness. When we lose that perspective, we can struggle with forgiving others. Jesus specifically warns about this phenomenon in the parable of the unmerciful servant.

You might remember that the parable (Matthew 18:21–35) starts with Peter approaching Jesus and asking just how many times he should forgive when he has been sinned against. Seven times? No, seventy times seven. Then Jesus explains: A king decided to settle accounts. A certain man owed him the equivalent of several million dollars. Since he could not possibly pay such a vast sum back, the king "ordered that he and his wife and his children and all that he had be sold to repay the debt." The debtor fell to his knees and begged for mercy. Amazingly, the king took pity on him and canceled *all* his debt! Well, you can imagine how that debtor must have felt. Relief doesn't begin to capture his emotions. He was free! His wife and children were safe! He must have been overflowing with joy.

On his way out of this meeting with the king, he runs into a neighbor who owes him the equivalent of five bucks. So what does he do? He starts screaming at him to pay up! He grabs him and starts to choke him. This neighbor falls to his knees and begs for mercy, not even asking to have the debt forgiven, just pleading, "Be patient with me, and I will pay you back." Nothing doing. The guy had his neighbor thrown in jail.

The king hears about this and is furious. "You wicked servant," he says, "I canceled all that debt of yours because you begged me to. *Shouldn't you have had mercy on your fellow servant just as I had on you?*" Then, in anger, the king had him thrown in jail until that huge debt was repaid—a life sentence.

Jesus sums up the parable and says, "This is how my heavenly Father will treat each of you unless you forgive your brother *from your heart.*"

How to Forgive From the Heart

Forgiving another for a sin or an offense is not a feeling or a hopeful thought. Forgiving another is an action of the will with the power of the Holy Spirit. There are six steps that combine the will of the mind with prayer that every Christian can use to forgive another.

1. **Quiet your heart.** Settle your thoughts, calm your mind. Intentionally choose this time to forgive another. Allow yourself to focus solely on God and the forgiveness issue.
2. **Let the person, the hurt, the offense, or the sin come to mind.** Again, this is intentional. Allow yourself to focus on the situation. On the other hand, don't go rooting around in your mind for something to remember. You don't want to scour your mind looking for some overlooked hurt, offense, or sin. If you need to forgive another, the Holy Spirit will gently bring it to your mind.

It's important that you don't censor yourself here. I specifically included hurts and offenses, as well as sins, in this step. If you have an emotional response to a situation, almost always you need to forgive the other person. Squeezing the toothpaste tube from the middle or leaving dirty laundry on the floor may not be sin, but it can be offensive, maybe even hurtful. Sometimes we censor ourselves and never get to forgiveness by thinking, *I shouldn't let this bother me, it's such a little thing,* or *No wonder she said that, look at what she's going through,* or *She really didn't mean to hurt me, it's just her way.* Making excuses for someone's behavior is not the same thing as forgiving them.

Then, very important, allow the emotion associated with the event to come to mind. This may not be pleasant, but it is critical. Identify the emotion. Is it betrayal? Hurt feelings? Frustration? Abandonment?

3. **Pray.** Specifically and intentionally forgive the other person for the hurt, offense, or sin *and* the emotional reaction it brought up in you. Your prayer could be short and straightforward: "Heavenly Father, when Sally told Jane that I am struggling with anger over my teenage daughter's attitude and that I am worried about her faith, I felt betrayed. I told Sally this in confidence, as my Bible study teacher. She broke my trust. She hurt me. Yet your Word says I am to forgive her. Please pour out your Spirit into my soul and help me to forgive her. Oh, God, I forgive Sally. In Jesus' name, amen."

4. **Continue praying.** Confess any sin you may have committed as a result of this hurt, offense, or sin against you. Is there any prejudice or wrong attitude you've had because of this situation? Once again, don't go ruthlessly searching through your past. If there's something for you to confess, God's own Spirit will bring it to your mind. Following the

example from step three, you might pray, "Lord, because of Sally's betrayal, I've never really trusted other Bible study teachers. I have assumed that they were all untrustworthy. I confess this prejudice and bad attitude to you. Please forgive me. In Jesus' name, amen."

5. **Thank God.** Trust His work in you through your obedience. Believe that you have forgiven and have been forgiven. Do not rely on your feelings. Using 1 John 1:9, you might pray, "Dear Lord, I have confessed my sins. You are faithful and just. You have forgiven me of my sins. You are purifying me from all unrighteousness. I believe this, regardless of how I feel. Amen."

6. **Repeat as necessary.** Some hurts or sins go deeper than others. One time through these steps may be all that you need for a certain situation. Other situations require new levels of forgiveness. Think of a bruised onion. Sometimes the black bruise is on several layers. As each black layer is removed, the diameter of the bruise, the intensity of the bruise, decreases. After you have forgiven the person, assume that the forgiveness is complete and there are no underlying bruises. Then, if you find there is still an emotional response in you, or if you are still not at peace about this situation, start the six-step process again. You may find that the emotion you identify in step two changes while you're praying. God will reveal what the underlying issues are so we can truly forgive. He equips and empowers us to forgive. We need only walk in faith and choose to forgive.

Leave Room for God

Forgiving isn't letting the other person off the hook. It's not being a doormat and letting everyone walk all over you and hurt you. Forgiveness is an act of faith. When we forgive another person, we are agreeing with God that a wrong has been committed. And then we let God be the Judge. We leave room for God's justice and His vengeance. God's Word is clear on this point. In three different places He says, "It is mine to avenge; I will repay" (Deuteronomy 32:35; Romans 12:19; and Hebrews 10:30). Will we believe this? Will we trust God when we've been hurt, offended, or even sinned against?

There is a strong probability that many of the women reading this have been sinned against sexually. Horribly violated and deeply wounded, often by people that they trusted, and who should have been their protectors. I am so sorry. How can such acts ever be forgiven? Only by the grace of God.

Why would God demand forgiveness in such a situation? Surely if there was ever a reason not to forgive, sexual crimes or murder must be good reasons. And yet, they are not. God does not require forgiveness in only certain situations; He requires forgiveness in every situation (Matthew 6:14–15, 18:25; Mark 11:25; Luke 6:37; Colossians 3:13). The results of unforgiveness are so catastrophic for the Christian (a life of bitterness, prejudices, sin, and utter defeat) that God's command to forgive is emphatic.

Once more, will we believe God? Will we trust that His way is best? Can we trust Him with our deepest hurts? Do we believe that God is trustworthy? His actions invite us to trust Him: "But because of his great love for us, God, who is rich in mercy, made us alive with Christ even when we were dead in transgressions—it is by grace you have been saved" (Ephesians 2:4–5).

And here is our model for forgiveness: "You see, at just the right time, when we were still powerless, Christ died for the ungodly. Very rarely will anyone die for a righteous man, though for a good person someone might possibly dare to die. But God demonstrates his own love for us in this: While we were still sinners, Christ died for us" (Romans 5:6–8). We were forgiven before we even knew we had sinned. We did not apologize or acknowledge our wrongs. God did not wait for us to realize our sins, to apologize, to show remorse, or to beg for forgiveness. He forgave. He forgives still.

Prayer Support

In the Sermon on the Mount, Jesus addressed the topic of fasting and said,

> When you fast, do not look somber as the hypocrites do, for they disfigure their faces to show others they are fasting. Truly I tell you, they have received their reward in full. But when you fast, put oil on your head and wash your face, so that it will not be obvious to others that you are fasting, but only to your Father, who is unseen; and your Father, who sees what is done in secret, will reward you. (Matthew 6:16–18)

Is Jesus saying that all fasting must be done in secret? No. Just like His other teachings concerning prayer, giving, and fasting, He is addressing the heart and telling us:

Don't be a hypocrite.

Don't turn the internal, Spirit-led work of fasting into an external work of the flesh.

Don't boast about fasting.

Humbly seeking prayer support for a fast, especially a long fast, is not hypocritical; it is wise.

I always ask my husband to pray for me when I fast for more than twenty-four hours. I also ask my children to pray for me. On longer fasts, I have asked for prayer support, usually from two or three people. As you are preparing to fast, pray about your prayer support. Certain fasts lend themselves to seeking prayer support. You may be fasting for a prodigal child or for a missions trip or for revival and, like Esther, you want your brothers and sisters to join you in prayer while you fast (Esther 4:15–17). Ask. You won't be a hypocrite, and God will reward you for obeying Him.

CHAPTER 5

(en)During the Fast

For you have need of endurance, so that when you have done the will of God, you may receive what is promised.

—*Hebrews 10:36 (NRSV)*

The questions and concerns I hear most often about fasting are, "I think I might be called to fast, but I'm not sure if I can do it;" "What if I start and don't finish?" "What if it's just too hard?" The thought of starting a fast and then not finishing it keeps many women from ever fasting at all. The idea of not eating for hours, days, or weeks can be a little frightening. The truth is, anyone who is called to fast can complete a liquids-only fast with good preparation and some knowledge of what to expect.

Since fasting has both a physical and spiritual aspect, successful fasting requires recognizing the challenges that each aspect brings to fasting. During a fast, the physical aspects are the most challenging. After the fast, the spiritual aspects are the most challenging.

What to Expect During a Fast

Each person's fast is unique. I am presenting some common fasting experiences in this chapter. You may or may not experience all of these and maybe not in this order. Some people find their first twenty-four-hour fast far easier than they expected. They report that they were hardly hungry. Other people find that fasting is harder than they thought it would be. They are shocked to find that they were really hungry from 10 a.m. to 5 p.m., when they eagerly ended the fast. Some people have big spiritual breakthroughs or mountaintop feelings; others feel like the fast is a slog and they are simply obeying God.

For partial fasts, the physical challenges will be different. Notice I didn't say easier; they are challenging in their own way. Not eating a food that you regularly eat will not be easy. Expect spiritual benefits and deeper intimacy with God whether the fast is liquids only or partial.

Twenty-Four-Hour Fasts

Sometimes women are surprised at how hungry they are during a fast. The strong focus on the spiritual aspects of fasting often leaves a person with little understanding of the physical aspects of fasting. Trust me, you'll be hungry. Recognize and accept that it's perfectly natural and normal to be hungry when you don't eat.

When you're hungry, drink. It's really important to drink often, usually every two to three hours. Be careful to sip, not gulp. Fasting often brings hiccups and burping; gulping just makes it worse. What to drink? Since you're not fasting long enough for your digestive system to go into a resting phase, almost any liquid will work. The strong recommendation to avoid all proteins and fats doesn't apply to a twenty-four-hour fast because your digestive system is not going to be at rest and you don't need to be concerned about bringing it out of the resting state.

All the liquids I recommended in chapters 1 and 4 apply here (broth, Campbell's tomato soup, etc.). Also, as I recommended earlier, drink coffee if you're a coffee drinker (mindful of the diuretic property of caffeine), or Pepsi, or whatever you normally drink.

You will discover which liquids work best for you. If I drink too much plain water on an empty stomach, I feel nauseated. I usually mix plain water or seltzer water with a little cranberry juice. Plain tomato soup is a wonderful lunch break; I drink it out of a large mug.

You won't want to be too far from the bathroom. All this increased drinking plus the natural loss of water weight means increased urination. Don't be surprised if your urine is nearly clear. If it's not clear or light yellow, you may not be drinking enough. The fastest way to fail at fasting is to not drink enough.

You may have headaches. If you started fasting the evening before, this might come on around lunchtime. After years of frequent fasting headaches, I finally realized that taking Tylenol (acetaminophen) doesn't break a fast! I avoid aspirin and ibuprofen because they are best taken with food, but acetaminophen works really well for me. No more fasting headaches. Fasting can also trigger migraines. That has happened to me a few times, but never with a twenty-four hour fast and usually because I have not fasted well. If you are susceptible to migraines, you *must* rest, in addition to drinking a lot. Every time I've gotten a migraine during a fast (and it's only been a few times), it's because I wasn't resting enough and/or I became dehydrated. I take an over-the-counter migraine medicine, and if I'm smart enough to take it as soon as I feel the migraine coming on, I have complete relief.

Expect loud rumblings and gurgling from your stomach. Take that as a signal to drink some more. You may feel tired and a little cold, especially toward the end of the twenty-four hours. You may think about food. A lot. When food thoughts come into my mind, I often repeat Matthew 5:6: "Blessed are those who hunger and thirst for righteousness, for they will be filled." It acknowledges that I am hungry and reminds me why I am fasting. If I dwell on food too much, I'll actually feel hungrier.

What to do about social events or when you're offered food while fasting? I cover this a bit later in the section on fasting for four to seven days, but let me just mention here that no one is as aware as you are that you are not eating. I am often able to adjust my schedule so I can avoid a social situation or just adjust the fast. For instance, I may plan a twenty-four-hour fast and then get an invitation to lunch from an old friend. I may just go to lunch and start the fast after lunch, skip dinner and breakfast, and break the fast with lunch the following day. We are fasting under grace, not law. When we are seeking God and spending extra time with Him, the order of the meals skipped doesn't matter.

When you first start fasting, you may be focused on the not-eating aspect. The idea that you could really go for a whole day without eating solid foods may make you a little apprehensive. As the day progresses and you keep your fast, you may start to feel a little confident. And then, about two hours before the twenty-four hours are up, it hits you. You are not feeling confident and strong; you're feeling hungry, tired, and cranky. You may be short-tempered or easily annoyed. Don't panic. The fast is working right on schedule.

After we've just devoted extra time in prayer and in the Word, we might be caught off-guard when, all of a sudden, an ugly thought pops into our head or a mean-spirited remark spews out from our mouth. Richard Foster describes this phenomenon in his chapter on fasting in *Celebration of Discipline:*

> More than any other Discipline, fasting reveals the things that control us. This is a wonderful benefit to the true disciple who longs to be transformed into the image of Jesus Christ. We cover up what is inside us with food and other good things, but in fasting these things surface. If pride controls us, it will be revealed almost immediately. David said, "I humbled my soul with fasting" (Ps. 69:10). Anger, bitterness, jealousy, strife, fear—if they are within us, they will surface during fasting. At first we will rationalize that our anger is due to our hunger; then we know that we are angry because the spirit of anger is within us. We can rejoice in this knowledge because we know that healing is available through the power of Christ.[1]

This is precisely why we are fasting: to reveal the true condition of our hearts and be healed, redeemed, and transformed. These negative spiritual experiences don't mean that your fast went wrong; they show you that your fast is going right.

Two- to Three-Day Fasts

By the second day of a fast, your tongue will be pasty, with a yellowish-greenish coating. If you didn't have a headache on the first day, you may get one on the second day. On the second or third day, you may start to feel lightheaded, especially when you stand or sit up quickly. You may feel like you need to go to bed at 8 p.m. on the second day, and that's after resting at 2:30 in the afternoon. This is all perfectly normal. It's also normal if you have none of these experiences. You may feel more energized and feel like you need less sleep.

You may have bad breath and a stronger body odor. In a two- to three-day fast, your digestive system is starting to slow down. By the third day, you may notice that your taste changes. The coffee you drank happily on the first two days may taste awful to you now. Or you may drink coffee throughout your fast. You may feel cold, particularly in your hands and feet. By the second night, I have to wear socks to bed, even if the fast is in the middle of the summer. Not a pretty sight, but there it is.

You may feel like you can't concentrate; like your brain is in a fog. This does not last, but it's often most severe on the third day. Keep drinking mostly clear liquids every two to three hours. Your body is adjusting to the fast and you will have lost any extra water weight by the third day; your trips to the bathroom will be much less.

I wish I could say I was all sweetness and light, constantly cheerful, when I fast. Sometimes I get cranky—I'm tired, hungry, and maybe fighting a headache. Actually, I don't even need to be fasting to be cranky and ill-tempered! Although I find I have better self-control when I am fasting, I still have had to apologize for being short-tempered with my family. Mostly, I avoid this by asking for help. Even when my children were small, my four-year-old could understand that I needed to rest and she needed to play quietly while her little brother napped. Prayer support is invaluable at times like this. Call someone and ask for prayer.

Spiritually, you may be stunned at how powerfully God's Word speaks to you. You may have a renewed hunger to read your Bible and find yourself devouring chapter after chapter. When Satan came to tempt Jesus after His forty-day fast, he said:

"If you are the Son of God, tell these stones to become bread." Jesus answered, "It is written: 'Man shall not live on bread alone, but on every word that comes from the mouth of God'" (Matthew 4:3–4).

When you're fasting, the Word is food for your soul. It is nourishment in a way that food can never be.

I have found that a three-day, liquids-only fast is particularly powerful. The combination of fasting that is hard physically (you don't reach the euphoric feeling that fasting for long periods can bring—for the most part you'll deal with hunger each day), with the added prayer time and time in the Word, is very effective. Not to exaggerate, you will suffer during a three-day fast. Dallas Willard writes, "In fasting, we learn how to suffer happily as we feast on God. And it is a good lesson, because in our lives we *will* suffer, no matter what else happens to us. Thomas à Kempis remarks: 'Whosoever knows best how to suffer will keep the greatest peace. That man is conqueror of himself, and lord of the world, the friend of Christ, and heir of Heaven.'"[2] Fasting teaches us to suffer happily, to learn the truth of Paul's statement, "I consider that our present sufferings are not worth comparing with the glory that will be revealed in us" (Romans 8:18).

Four- to Seven-Day Fasts

By the fourth day, the coating on your tongue may start to disappear. It's usually gone by the seventh day. Your energy level may pick up a little, or you may be fatigued. The confused mental fog feeling is often gone by the seventh day. In fact, you may start to feel mentally alert and vibrantly aware of your surroundings. Often, after the third day, I am filled with excitement and renewed energy.

It's critical to keep drinking very regularly.[3] Your digestion is starting to slow down to a resting state. Your hunger pains may be greatly diminished and may be completely gone by now. Or not.

You may have a generalized, low-level hunger feeling with only a few hunger pains. Here's when you get a little over-confident and stop drinking every two to three hours. Don't. Stay on your drinking schedule.

By this point you'll want to avoid chewing gum, mints, or anything that may stimulate your salivary glands. Salivation is the first step in the digestive process. You will want to avoid anything that stimulates your digestion. The liquids you drink should not have any animal protein or fat.

You may begin to feel like you're in a spiritual bubble, a very safe, secure, peaceful place. Deep feelings of hope and joy may wash over you. You may have a pervasive sense of peace. When I read my journals, I am amazed at how many times I use the word hope, especially that I am filled with hope. You may start to feel that you're in the world but not of the world. Your prayer life intensifies and you may be drawn into more intercession.

Depending on your faith tradition, you may celebrate the Lord's Supper or Communion regularly or weekly. How does the bread or wafer and the juice or wine fit into fasting? Perfectly. Fasting is communion and intimacy with God. I have never felt that I could not participate in the fellowship of communion while fasting. Even in longer fasts, the small piece of bread or wafer has never been an issue. Truthfully, Communion is especially meaningful when I am fasting; the spiritual element outweighs the physical element.

When fasting for more than three days, it's likely that you may run into social situations that include food. Because you are so aware that you are not eating, you might think everyone else will notice that you're not eating. Not even close. I have gone to several social events while fasting and no one ever noticed. Unless it is a sit-down, formal event, you can usually just drink your way through it. If I'm invited to a restaurant meal or something formal while fasting, I politely decline. I don't lie, and I almost never need to say that I'm fasting. I might say that I'd love to come but it doesn't fit into my schedule that day (true, because it doesn't fit into my fasting schedule, but I don't need to share all of that). On the other hand, I have gone to restaurants with Christian friends who knew I was fasting and I just ordered iced tea or water.

One challenge of fasting for a longer period is cooking for others. When I was first called to fast, my children were two and four years old. It seemed I spent most of each day in the kitchen getting juices, snacks, and meals. That didn't stop when I started a fast. I came to realize that although I was called to fast, I was first called to be a wife to my husband and a mother to my children. The call to fast didn't negate those previous calls.

When I am fasting, I still cook dinner for my family most nights and do laundry and all the other things I normally do. I can only attribute it to God's grace. It's a joke in my family that I make some of the best meals when I'm fasting—meals that I regularly prepare come out "the best ever, Mom!" when I'm cooking without tasting. Again, I'm sure it's all God's grace. I still carpool to various activities and help with homework. I think of it this way: I was called to fast (with its sacrifices); they were not. Yet, some days, I am really tired and making dinner just isn't going to happen. Since my family knows I am fasting and I don't give up cooking for days and days, they manage. I've been known to order pizza or drive through a fast-food restaurant—which thrills them to no end.

One blessing of having prayer supporters in a long fast has been meals for my family. More than once, dinner has been provided for my family while I have been fasting. I can still remember a meal delivered in 1999 at just the right time. I never asked for the meal; God prompted her heart and she obeyed. We were both blessed.

I'm often asked about fasting and physical intimacy in marriage. Scripture is clear on this:

> The wife does not have authority over her own body but yields it to her husband. In the same way, the husband does not have authority over his own body but yields it to his wife. Do not deprive each other except perhaps by mutual consent and for a time, so that you may devote yourselves to prayer. Then come together again so that Satan will not tempt you because of your lack of self-control. (1 Corinthians 7:4–5)

One person's call to fast is not necessarily mutual consent. I don't see how a wife declaring to her husband that she's been called to fast, and there will be no sexual relations for forty days, blesses any marriage.

EIGHT- TO TWENTY-ONE-DAY FASTS

After one week of fasting, your digestive system is coming to a full resting state. The hunger pains are replaced by a generalized, low-level hunger. It may feel like a dull, empty feeling. Or you may not feel hungry at all. You're likely aware of food but not tempted. If you are still hungry and think about eating all the time, that's normal, too. You're not any less spiritual; you're not doing the fast wrong. Every person's metabolism is different; some people are done with hunger by the fourth day, some by the fourteenth, and some never hit that loss-of-hunger feeling.

You may notice that you look healthier, especially your skin, hair, and nails. Your physical energy and mental acuity are much better. You may feel like your mind is sharp and focused. Your energy level is probably steadier; you may not have that afternoon dip in energy. I often feel like I've turned a corner on the tenth day—less hunger and more energy. However, it's important that you conserve energy. Take every opportunity to rest. Although you may be feeling better, you are operating at an energy deficit. Don't over-schedule yourself, and keep up your drinking schedule.

You may notice that you feel cold most of the time. This is the point in a fast when I'm most susceptible to foot cramps because my feet are so cold. Drink warm liquids and bundle up. Another thing, you may notice that your bowel movements are infrequent, or they may be daily but more watery. There's a difference between diarrhea, a clear signal to STOP fasting, and a diarrhea-like bowel movement. In a liquids-only fast, it is not uncommon to have a watery bowel movement. I have been told that people who fast with water only stop having bowel movements completely, a normal occurrence with nothing going through the digestive system.

This may be one of the most profound spiritual times in your life. More than once I have had clear direction from God at this point in a fast. This does not happen every time I fast, but it does happen often. It was the twentieth day of a fast when God revealed my food idol to me and set me free. September 11, 2001, occurred on the twelfth day of a fast. Another time I was fasting for twenty-one days and had a huge breakthrough on self-discipline. On the thirteenth day of that fast I wrote:

> Oh! The depths of the riches and grace of my God! He opened my eyes and revealed to me what He is doing for me in this fast . . . giving me discipline! I have always wanted to be self-disciplined and have not felt that self-control I yearned for. As I was praying about this fast being harder, as far as being hungry, the Holy Spirit just completely opened my eyes! He is giving me the disciplined life so that I can be free in Christ.

Indescribable hope. I can be disciplined because I am exercising self-discipline now and throughout this fast.

The discipline of fasting has taught me (is teaching me still) to be a disciplined person. The Holy Spirit is using this discipline to produce in me the fruit of self-control. Dallas Willard captures this connection between fasting and self-control in his book *The Spirit of the Disciplines*.[4] He writes, "Fasting teaches temperance or self-control and therefore teaches moderation and restraint with regard to *all* our fundamental drives." I have found this to be true. Denying our flesh through fasting helps us to deny our flesh when the fast is over.

Thirty- to Forty-Day Fasts

Your digestive system remains at rest during a fast of this length. Your energy level may start to drop again. Afternoon rests may become necessary once more. You may feel cold all the time. At this point, I might get cold enough to shiver. If that happens, I pile on the blankets, drink something warm, and rest for fifteen to twenty minutes. You'll need to be careful to keep drinking. During this time in a fast, you may slip into a little laziness, just drinking when you feel like it. Please don't. If anything, increase your drinking to keep your energy level up.

Food thoughts may be coming into your mind regularly. You may have cravings for particular foods. I often start desiring high-fat foods at this point. It's normal for your body to crave fats and proteins; you are depleted in those areas. When those thoughts come to me, I pray something like, "I hunger and thirst for you, O Lord. I know that those who hunger and thirst for righteousness will be satisfied. Food will never satisfy me; only you satisfy me, Lord Jesus. Amen." I also sing the line from a contemporary Christian song[5] by Kathryn Scott that was popular a few years back: "Hungry, I come to you, for I know you satisfy." I repeat this and the food thoughts disappear—until they come back. There is nothing unspiritual about this. It is a regular occurrence in fasting. Perseverance is key.

One really important warning: If true hunger returns, you need to end the fast. True hunger will feel like the sharp hunger pains you had in the first few days of the fast. Instead of the dull, empty, low-level hunger feeling, it is an insistent, sharp hunger pain. It's different from what you've been experiencing physically. Do not ignore this; do not gut through this. End your fast. This has happened to me only once. I was going to end a forty-day fast at 5 p.m. on Palm Sunday. By noon, I was hungry, shaky, and nauseated. I remember praying and asking God to let me finish, and His answer to my spirit was, "You are finished." I broke the fast and had complete peace. I learned that because God ordained the fast, He can end it any time. It is finished when He says it is—not by the clock on the wall or a date on the calendar.

When we fast, we are obeying God's call. We faithfully seek His will, asking how long we should fast, what kind of a fast it should be, and what to pray about during the fast. Then we may start fasting with the idea that we have all the answers and absolutely know why we're fasting. I am often guilty of this. Yet in every fast, I end up praying about something I didn't even know about when I started the fast. God is in complete control. When He is satisfied with our fast, He will end it. The tricky part is recognizing God's command to end the fast versus our desire to end a fast and go back to eating. It requires inviting the Holy Spirit to search and examine your heart. In my case, it was such a markedly different physical feeling that I knew it was about my body, not my flesh. I desired to do the will of God with all my heart; He told me to end the fast. Obedience is the goal, not self-righteousness.

Another time I was fasting for fourteen days. On the eighth day I got strep throat. I had never gotten sick while fasting and have never since then. I was sick as a dog. I should have ended the fast at that point. Instead, I gutted it out, increased my soup intake, and finished the fourteen days. Stupid. You would think I would know better, that I would know that fasting is about the heart, not about legalistically fasting for a certain number of days! Instead, I had to learn, the hard way, that I had made fasting a little bit about me. I was so concerned about not failing at the call to fast, about finishing what I had started, that I started to worship fasting instead of God. Yikes. Really, really stupid.

Fasting is not a legalistic ritual; it is a wholehearted response to God. It is a desire to pursue Him, to please and delight Him and so be transformed. Start the fast with prayerful preparation. Assume you have heard the call to fast, the length of the fast, and the type of fast correctly. Trust that God will guide you. And if the guidance is to end the fast, obey God. Don't let the idea that you have answered the call to fast and have made a vow to the Lord that must not be broken (Numbers 30:2) keep you from the grace of God. If you are unsure about God's guidance, ask your husband and your prayer support partners. When we seek God with all of our heart, He will be found. The goal is God, not forty days or twenty-four hours of fasting.

THE HEART OF FASTING

Since fasting is about wholeheartedly following and pursuing God, the question becomes, How do we do that? We know it's more than just not eating. The answer is, we follow and pursue God in His Word, the Bible.

Many years ago I attended a retreat, and the speaker taught us how to listen to God as we read the Bible. I had been reading the Bible, studying the Bible, and even memorizing the Bible, but I had never been taught to *hear* the Bible. I started to practice what she taught, simplified and tweaked it a bit, and have never looked back.

Listening to God

When we read the Bible, we learn about who God is, who the Holy Spirit is, who Jesus is, and the way of salvation. We learn about what pleases and delights God. We learn about His good character, His steadfastness, and His mercy. The Bible is God's perfect and complete truth. Yet when we're listening for God, the Bible isn't only God's Holy Word full of truth; the Bible becomes an individual love letter to us. The same Holy Spirit who inspired the writers of the Bible will speak to us as we listen for Him while we read the Bible.

How do we hear what the Spirit is saying? This will sound obvious, but we have to learn to listen. First, we start with faith:

Without faith it is impossible to please God, because anyone who comes to him must believe that he exists and that he rewards those who earnestly seek him. (Hebrews 11:6)

Then we believe He speaks to us and we can know His voice:

"The one who enters by the gate is the shepherd of the sheep. The gatekeeper opens the gate for him, and the *sheep listen to his voice. He calls his own sheep by name* and leads them out. When he has brought out all his own, he goes on ahead of them, and *his sheep follow him because they know his voice.* But they will never follow a stranger; in fact, they will run away from him because they do not recognize a stranger's voice." Jesus used this figure of speech, but the Pharisees did not understand what he was telling them. Therefore Jesus said again, "Very truly I tell you,

I am the gate for the sheep. . . . I am the good shepherd; *I know my sheep and my sheep know me*—just as the Father knows me and I know the Father—and I lay down my life for the sheep. I have other sheep that are not of this sheep pen. I must bring them also. *They too will listen to my voice,* and there shall be one flock and one shepherd" (John 10: 2–7, 14–16).

Finally, we can start reading with listening ears.

Here are the six steps I use to hear God in my daily quiet time. Modify this any way that works for you.

1. Start with the expectation that God will speak to you with His Spirit through His Word. Jesus is your shepherd and you are one of His sheep.
2. Be still. Quiet your heart. Pray, and ask God to open the eyes of your heart so that you can hear what He is saying to you.
3. Start reading. As you read, be aware of the verse (or word, phrase, or passage) that:

   leaps off the page, or
   strikes you, or
   gives you pause, or
   arrests your attention, or
   requires you to read it over again, or
   gives you an "aha" moment, or
   directly answers a concern of your heart.

   Many of us have these experiences when we read the Bible; we just didn't know it was the gentle voice of the Spirit speaking to our spirit. We thought it was merely an interesting verse or wonderfully comforting word. We may have even stopped and wondered about it before we continued on with our Bible reading. Yet this is how the Spirit speaks through the Word of God; He stirs your soul and your mind as you spend time in His Word.

4. Write it down. Write down the verse (or word, phrase, or passage) that you just heard.

5. Pray. Starting with the Word you just heard, talk to God about it. Sometimes you'll know exactly what God is saying to you, other times you'll know as soon as you pray. Sometimes you may not know what the verse means until later. Write down what you heard in prayer, the thoughts that came to you. Write down any prayer-response to what you heard.

6. End your time with thanksgiving, praise, and worship, acknowledging that God loves you, knows you, and speaks to you.

You may be thinking this is too complicated or that it takes too much time. I promise you, it's really doable. In fact, when I teach these steps to women's groups, within ten minutes most women hear God speak to them, write down their verse, and pray. Honest. Some people need more time and a little more practice recognizing God's voice in His Word. God is faithful; He will guide you. If it takes you a little longer, it doesn't mean you're not spiritual or a good Christian. Give it a little practice and trust God. Your quiet times will be so rich that I anticipate you'll use this method even when you're not fasting. Let me share how this works in real life.

I really like to read through the Bible in a year. I find that reading from Genesis to Revelation, year after year, opens my eyes to the full counsel of God's Word. I can't recommend this enough. I have several One Year Bibles in various translations and formats. I read either the regular One Year Bible, with a passage from the Old Testament, the New Testament, a psalm, and a proverb each day, or I use the One Year Chronological Bible (which is especially helpful with the Kings, Chronicles, and the Prophets). As much as I like One Year Bibles, I always pray about what Bible to use in the New Year. One year I spent the entire year in the New Testament. This year I've been reading a chronological Bible and stopping each day at the verse that speaks to me. Some days I barely read a verse or two before I hear the voice of my Lord; other days I might read several pages before I hear the Word for me. The best part is that God is always faithful. He speaks to His children so that we can know His voice and know Him.

If I am reading through the Bible in a year, I read the whole day's selection. When I come across the verse that pops off of the page and speaks to my heart, I note it and keep reading the rest of the selection. Then I write down the verse and start praying. Here's a sample from one of my journals:

> 1 Samuel 12:22 "... because the Lord was <u>pleased to make you his own</u>." (I underlined the emphasis I heard when I read the verse.)
>
> In Jesus, God has made me His own. He bought me, redeemed me, and chose me. He loves me with an everlasting love.

This is the entire entry. I am not writing pages and pages every day. Sometimes an important word or phrase is so obvious I simply underline it. Other times I write what God spoke to me about the verse along with my prayer back to Him. And sometimes I write down the verse or phrase and just my prayer-response to it.

Usually when you hear the verse, you know what it means for you. Those of us who are mothers sometimes forget that God is full of love and mercy, and we're waiting to hear God speak to us in the "mom" voice. You know that voice; it's the one our kids hear when we're telling them to clean up their rooms. Again. But

God speaks tenderly to His beloved children. Even when we have just confessed to Him a sin, He is full of compassion and love.

Every once in a while I hear a verse and obediently write it down, and I have no idea what it means for me. Even after praying. A few years ago I heard the following verse: "But he knows the way that I take; when *he has tested me,* I will come forth as gold" (Job 23:10). I didn't feel like I was under any test, so my entire journal entry was just this verse—no thoughts, no prayer-response.

The next day's journal entry started with this: "I wasn't sure what yesterday's verse meant when I heard it and wrote it. By last night it was the most comforting and powerful Word I've ever heard from my Lord!" A sister in Christ called me up and accused me of something that I did not do, but I chose to forgive her and love her. When I hung up the phone, I was a bit shaken. As I sat down to pray, the verse from Job *immediately* came to mind. God was telling me that I was tested and He was pronouncing me innocent. Tears of joy flooded my eyes. I believe that the Lord could so quickly bring it to my mind so that I could receive His great comfort, because I didn't merely read it, I wrote it down.

Journaling

You may have wonderful quiet times in sweet fellowship with our Lord now. You may hear His voice in prayer regularly. But when you write it down, you create a personal testimony of God's faithfulness. It's incredibly powerful to look back and see the hand of God at work in your life. The big things we remember; a journal captures the thousand small things that our faithful God does for us all the time.

I became a believer in journaling many years ago during the *Experiencing God* Bible study I mentioned previously. The study featured daily homework, ending with the opportunity to write down the most significant sentence or phrase from that day's lesson and our response to it. Halfway through the study, we were instructed to go back and reread all of our responses. I was blown away. God was speaking clearly to me; an obvious pattern emerged, but I never saw it until I read the responses over the previous six weeks all together. I never wanted to miss another word from God again.

If the only journaling you do is when you fast, you will be blessed. In addition to the spiritual truths you're gleaning, your journal is a great place to keep track of what works for you while you fast. I came to realize the effects of apple juice on me (not pretty) because I saw the pattern in my journal.

When I first started using this listening and journaling method in my quiet times, I thought a binder filled with loose-leaf paper and separate tabs for prayer lists, journaling, and Bible verses would be good. Way too complicated for me. You may need to experiment a bit until you find a system that works best for you. A binder system may be perfect for you. I find that a small spiral-bound notebook, similar in size to my Bible, works best for me. I keep a pen right inside the spiral coils and can often fit the notebook inside my Bible case. Nothing will end journaling faster than having to hunt for the notebook and pen every time.

Meditating on God's Word

Meditation is a widespread practice throughout the Bible, noted particularly in the Psalms. Yet because Eastern and mystical religions practice a non-biblical form of meditation, many Christians seem to shy away from this worthy discipline.

There are two opposing methods of meditation. The Eastern, mystical method strives for the mind to be emptied. This is just plain dangerous. Run, flee from anyone telling you to empty your mind, lose your consciousness, or let your mind just float. An empty mind is an invitation to the enemy. Jesus describes this in Matthew 12:43–45:

> When an impure spirit comes out of a person, it goes through arid places seeking rest and does not find it. Then it says, "I will return to the house I left." When it arrives, *it finds the house unoccupied, swept clean and put in order.* Then it goes and takes with it seven other spirits more wicked than itself, and they go in and live there. And the final condition of that person is worse than the first.

Biblical meditation is the complete opposite. We meditate to *fill* our minds with God's Word. This is so important that God commands it. When Joshua was first taking over leadership of the Israelites after Moses' death, God spoke to him and said,

> Keep this Book of the Law always on your lips; *meditate on it day and night,* so that you may be careful to do everything written in it. Then you will be prosperous and successful. (Joshua 1:8)

The Psalms are full of references to meditation and meditating, and each reference connects meditation to filling the mind with God and His Word. I recognize that some Christians are a little wary of the practice of meditation. I am including every verse about meditation below. They are short; please read through each one to be assured that meditation is biblical and godly.

> But whose delight is in the law of the Lord, and who meditates on his law day and night. (Psalm 1:2)

> May these words of my mouth and this meditation of my heart be pleasing in your sight, Lord, my Rock and my Redeemer. (Psalm 19:14)

> When I remember You on my bed, I meditate on You in the night watches. (Psalm 63:6 NASB)

I will consider all your works and meditate on all your mighty deeds. (Psalm 77:12)

I meditate on your precepts and consider your ways. (Psalm 119:15)

Though rulers sit together and slander me, your servant will meditate on your decrees. (Psalm 119:23)

I reach out for your commands, which I love, that I may meditate on your decrees. (Psalm 119:48)

May the arrogant be put to shame for wronging me without cause; but I will meditate on your precepts. (Psalm 119:78)

Oh, how I love your law! I meditate on it all day long. (Psalm 119:97)

I have more insight than all my teachers, for I meditate on your statutes. (Psalm 119:99)

My eyes stay open through the watches of the night, that I may meditate on your promises. (Psalm 119:148)

I remember the days of long ago; I meditate on all your works and consider what your hands have done. (Psalm 143:5)

They speak of the glorious splendor of your majesty—and I will meditate on your wonderful works. (Psalm 145:5)

How to Meditate

The *Renovaré Spiritual Formation Bible* defines *meditation* as "prayerful rumination upon God, his Word, and his world."[6] When I look up *ruminate* in Webster's, I find this definition: "chew cud; ponder over; meditate." The next definition is the word *rumination*: "quiet meditation and reflection." While we are fasting, we may not be eating bread, but we are living on God's Word. The connection between ruminating and pondering God's Word is particularly powerful when we're fasting. We experience Jesus' words that "man shall not live on bread alone, but on every word that comes from the mouth of God" (Matthew 4:4). Meditation is the thoughtful pondering, the slow chewing, of God's Word.

Like all disciplines, meditation requires practice. I recommend starting to meditate on the verse you heard God speak to you, either in your daily quiet time or the verse God gave you for your fast (while you were preparing to fast). Slowly repeat it to yourself. If you need to open your eyes and read it, go ahead. Keep repeating the verse slowly and mindfully. Think of each word. If one word or phrase is particularly meaningful, dwell on that.

Meditation is simply allowing God's Word to dwell within you. It's a method of intentionally feeding your soul. Start slow, maybe with a two-minute meditation session. If you find your mind is wandering and distracted, don't feel like you've failed. Try again. We've all learned to multitask so well that sometimes it's hard to be single-minded for any amount of time.

I find it helpful to start meditating by repeating the verse (or word or phrase) out loud a few times. I start with a normal voice and go down to a whisper and then to just saying the verse in my mind. The transition helps settle my mind. You may picture the words, or their meanings, in your mind. I recently meditated on a verse I heard in my daily prayer time, Psalm 62:6: "Truly he is my rock and my salvation; he is my fortress, I will not be shaken." At first I was focused on the words and repeating them in the right order. I had to open my eyes a few times to get the whole verse straight. Then, as I meditated, I saw a word picture. I focused my mind on the Rock and saw myself hidden within the cleft of a huge rock. I thought of salvation and felt a hopeful, heavenward feeling. I pictured a mighty, ancient, stone fortress surrounding me. The whole meditation was about God's faithfulness and His protection. I probably spent about five minutes meditating. But the verse and the sense of God's protection stayed with me all day long.

Why Meditate?

"Whatever is true, whatever is noble, whatever is right, whatever is pure, whatever is lovely, whatever is admirable—if anything is excellent or praiseworthy—think about such things" (Philippians 4:8). Meditation teaches us and trains us to think about such things.

When we meditate, we are focusing single-mindedly and wholeheartedly on God. It is a form of worship as we acknowledge God's worth with all of our minds. At the same time, we are inviting His Word to indwell us, to fill us. Meditation renews our minds from the old patterns of sinful thinking to new patterns of righteous thinking. Only a renewed mind can overcome the world and the flesh and live according to God's will (Romans 12:2). All transformation, all real change, comes from God's work within us.

Meditation is spending intimate, concentrated time alone with God. In Sarah Young's devotional *Jesus Calling*, she gives voice to God and the blessings that await those who do:

> Bring me the sacrifice of your time: a most precious commodity. In this action-addicted world, few of My children take time to sit quietly in My Presence. But for those who do, blessings flow like *streams of living water*. I, the One from whom all blessings flow, am also blessed by our time together. This is a deep mystery; do not try to fathom it. Instead, glorify Me by delighting in Me. Enjoy Me now and forever![7]

TRUST AND OBEY

Once we know what to do and what to expect in a fast, we can simply choose to trust and obey. Instead of being nervous or afraid of fasting, we can embrace the call of fasting in our lives. The old hymn "Trust and Obey"[8] ends with a verse that describes the joy I have found in following God with fasting. I pray it is your joy, too.

> Then in fellowship sweet
> we will sit at his feet,
> or we'll walk by his side in the way;
> what he says we will do,
> where he sends we will go;
> never fear, only trust and obey.

Refrain:

> Trust and obey, for there's no other way
> to be happy in Jesus, but to trust and obey.

CHAPTER 6

You Did It!

Well done, good and faithful servant! You have been faithful with a few things; I will put you in charge of many things. Come and share your master's happiness!

—Matthew 25:21

Congratulations! Whether the fast was for one meal or for forty days, you stuck with it and finished. I imagine your thoughts and feelings of gratitude to God are overflowing. Enjoy the sense of joy, the sweet sense of contentment. Savor the intimacy you have with the Lord.

Ending a fast well is as important as preparing for a fast. And like everything about fasting, there is both a physical and spiritual part to breaking the fast. In longer fasts, the proper breaking of the fast, physically and spiritually, is critical. Perhaps you've heard the same stories I have heard about people ending a fast by overeating and ending up in an emergency room with their stomachs being pumped. Just the thought of that scares me! That is not the norm. There is no reason to expect anything like that when you break your fast. The key to successfully breaking a fast is to reintroduce easily digestible foods very, VERY gradually.

BREAKING A ONE-MEAL TO ONE-DAY FAST

When ending a one-meal or one-day fast, you can break your fast with your next meal. There are no food restrictions, since your digestive system has not slowed down at all. Because you'll be hungry, the most important thing is to not eat too much when you start eating again. You don't want to start eating everything in sight. It takes as much discipline to end a fast well as it does to fast. The best thing is to eat just until your hunger is satisfied, not until you feel full. Think light meal, not Thanksgiving feast.

Most twenty-four-hour fasts start at the end of dinner, skip breakfast and lunch the next day, and break the fast with dinner. You will be no less spiritual if you end the fast with a delicious, favorite food. Sometimes I put something in the Crockpot in the morning knowing it will be ready when I am ready to eat.

BREAKING A TWO- TO THREE-DAY FAST

When you have fasted for one to two days, your digestive system has started to slow down, but it is not in a resting state. You can break your fast with your next meal and eat almost any food. If you have a sensitive stomach, avoid anything fried or greasy. The most important thing is not the type of food but the amount. Start slowly. Eat small amounts of food and let your hunger guide you. If you eat a little bit and you are still hungry, eat a little more. As soon as you feel food in your stomach, *long before you feel full,* stop eating.

Because you will be truly hungry, you may be surprised at how little food you eat before you feel food in your stomach. Put away any preconceived notions of how much food you can eat after fasting (and being truly hungry), and concentrate on when you feel food in your stomach, when your stomach is no longer empty. In other words, as soon as I can feel food in my stomach, even though I feel I could eat more (a lot more), I stop eating.

BREAKING A FOUR- TO SEVEN-DAY FAST

Your digestive system may or may not have entered into a resting state by the end of a four- to seven-day fast. If you have had consistent hunger throughout your fast, you most likely never slowed down to the resting phase. You can break the fast as described in the previous section ("Breaking a Two- to Three-Day Fast"). Be careful to eat small amounts, slowly.

If your hunger pains subsided, your digestive system was starting to slow down. You will want to carefully and gently reintroduce food. Start slowly with small amounts of food. Eat easily digestible foods to break your fast. Avoid fats and proteins for the first few meals. Keep your liquid intake high and add foods such as:

applesauce

bananas

plain toast

plain crackers (matzo or saltines)

rice

Jell-O

fruits

vegetables

After one or two days of easily digestible foods, you will be ready to add protein. Again, think of easily digestible proteins:

eggs

yogurt

cottage cheese

non-oily fish

Keep eating small amounts as you return to your normal diet.

BREAKING AN EIGHT- TO FORTY-DAY FAST

By the end of a liquids-only eight- to forty-day fast, your digestive system has slowed down to a resting state. It is really, really crucial to break your fast well. Dr. Don Colbert writes in *Fasting Made Easy,* "During your fast, your digestive tract has been at rest. It has not had to produce hydrochloric acid and pancreatic enzymes needed for digestion, so they will not be readily available at the end of the fast."[1] As you gradually reintroduce food in very small amounts, your digestive system will have the time to produce all that you need for healthy digestion. When you start to eat again, chew your food thoroughly. This is essential to start the salivary gland digestive process as well as to introduce well-chewed, soft food into the stomach.

The best comparison I have for this stage of a fast is introducing food to babies for the first time.

Think baby food: boiled, mashed, soft, and watery vegetables and fruits without any added sugar or salt. Think baby food amounts. We feed babies with a baby spoon, which is smaller than a regular teaspoon; a great visual cue for us when we're ending a fast. Think baby food jars, mere ounces. Start with small, small, small amounts of easily digestible vegetables and fruits.

Babies' taste buds are not yet developed; your taste buds may have reverted to a baby-like state during the fast. Even though I was juicing a carrot and apple mixture during my first forty-day fast, when I first ate I couldn't believe how sensitive my taste buds were. I tried to eat some grated raw carrots and cabbage. The carrots were amazingly sweet. The cabbage was like hot pepper! I could not tolerate it. I'm not kidding you; I had to spit it out.

If you end your fast at dinnertime, you might start with some soft vegetables. I discovered that canned, no-salt green beans are a great choice for me when I'm breaking a long fast. They are well cooked and soft. I open a small can and eat three or four beans. Really, three or four green beans, one at a time. I chew slowly and thoroughly. Then I wait. Within thirty to sixty minutes, I will feel hunger and want to eat. I have a few more beans. I won't even finish the can. All the while, I'll be drinking liquids. The next day, the second day of ending the fast, I might have some fruit. Watermelon is great. I avoid citrus fruits and starchy vegetables, like potatoes or corn. They are too hard to digest. During the second day I continue to eat soft vegetables and add fruit:

green beans or wax beans, canned or cooked well

carrots, canned or cooked well

squash

zucchini

banana

applesauce

Jell-O

By the third day, I can eat raw vegetables. I add starches:

toast, maybe with a little jam (no butter or margarine)

boiled potato

other starchy vegetables (but I still avoid corn)

rice

crackers

By lunch or dinner of this day I can usually add some easily digestible proteins:

cottage cheese

yogurt

scrambled eggs

I have found that imitation crab, sold as Louis Kemp Crab Delights, is a wonderful protein to start eating when breaking a long fast. As you fast, you will make your own discoveries of easily digestible foods that bless you as you reintroduce food into your body. I like fish, so imitation crab works for me. On the other hand, tuna fish, which is an oily fish, is way too strong for me. I treat tuna fish like a meat instead of a fish.

Usually by the fourth day I can add meats and fats. What I have found to be more important than what I eat is how much I eat. I have great success when I eat small amounts, slowly.

FROM THE MOUNTAINTOP TO THE DESERT?

You may have experienced a deep intimacy and a sweet fellowship with the Lord during your fast. The Word was more alive than ever; you heard the Lord speaking to you clearly, and your prayer life was vibrant. And then, all of a sudden, you feel like you've walked into a desert. After such a powerful spiritual experience, it's like the rug has been pulled out from under you. You are in great company—the same thing happened to Jesus.

Look at Luke's account of Jesus' forty-day fast:

When all the people were being baptized, Jesus was baptized too. And as he was praying, heaven was opened and the Holy Spirit descended on him in bodily form like a dove. And a voice came from heaven: "You are my Son, whom I love; with you I am well pleased." Now Jesus himself was about thirty years old when he began his ministry. He was the son, so it was thought, of Joseph. . . . Jesus, full of the Holy Spirit, left the Jordan and was led by the Spirit into the wilderness, where for forty days he was tempted by the devil. He ate nothing during those days, and at the end of them he was hungry. The devil said to him, "If you are the Son of God, tell this stone to become bread" (Luke 3:21–23; 4:1–3).

Don't miss this: It was at the *end of the fast* that the testing and tempting occurred. After Jesus had fasted for the forty days, He was equipped to resist the devil and prepared to start His ministry. There are three points that really strike me. First, Jesus was led to fast after He had a mountaintop experience, His baptism. Being called to fast does not mean you have some horrible sin or stronghold to overcome. God called Jesus to fast right after He spoke aloud from heaven and said that He loved Jesus and was well pleased with Him! Second, Jesus was tempted and overcame the temptation immediately after a successful fast; the fast itself was the preparation for the encounter with the devil. (I infer from Mark's account [1:12–13] that Jesus had a spiritually powerful fasting experience as well as a profound physical experience— wild animals did not hurt Him and the angels attended to Him.) Then, at the end of the forty days, He is tested and tempted by the devil himself, and Jesus overcomes each temptation with the Word of God. Third, right after this fast and test, Jesus starts His public ministry and selects the disciples.

Did you have an amazing spiritual time and now you feel like you're in the desert? Perhaps this desert experience is testing your heart. The very verse Jesus quoted in response to the devil's first temptation ("Man shall not live on bread alone," Luke 4:3–4) is from Deuteronomy 8:2–3:

> Remember how the Lord your God led you all the way in the wilderness these forty years, to humble you and to test you in order to know what was in your heart, whether or not you would keep his commands. He humbled you, causing you to hunger and then feeding you with manna, which neither you nor your ancestors had known, to teach you that man does not live on bread alone but on every word that comes from the mouth of the Lord.

Could God be equipping you to serve Him in a new way? Is He preparing your heart for ministry? Did your fast prepare you for a desert experience where you can show yourself strong in the Lord? Don't despair if you feel like you left the mountaintop and you're living in the desert. Trust that your fast has prepared you to be exactly where God would have you.

WALKING OUT THE VICTORY

One marvelous benefit of fasting is victory over our flesh. When we deny ourselves in fasting, we realize that we can deny ourselves in any other area. Fasting teaches us to serve God, and God alone. Jesus said, "No one can serve two masters. Either you will hate the one and love the other, or you will be devoted to the one and despise the other. You cannot serve both God and money" (Matthew 6:24). Fasting shows us who, or what, we really love. If our master is money, or food, or prestige, or whatever, it is revealed in a fast and we can choose to serve God wholeheartedly.

I saw my true spiritual condition when I realized that I loved food—that it was my master, an idol in the place of God—during my first forty-day fast. When the fast ended and I began to eat again, I continued to lose weight. Spiritually, I was eating food as sustenance, not as false worship. Physically, when I was breaking the fast, I learned how to eat just until I felt food in my stomach. I learned to eat as a person who serves God and not food.

Over the years I have caught myself slipping back into bad habits. When this happened the first time, I couldn't figure out what was going on. I had been set free from this idol, so why was food and overeating such a temptation all over again? As I prayed about this I've come to realize that the victory I had over this idol must be walked out in faith daily. After Jesus rebuffed the devil's third temptation, Luke writes, "When the devil had finished all this tempting, *he left him until an opportune time*" (4:15). Our enemy does not give up.

There is no victory apart from obedience. Not past obedience, only present obedience. Scripture is clear: We are slaves and we will serve a master. Obedience is choosing to be God's slave and not sin's slave:

> For we know that our old self was crucified with him so that the body ruled by sin might be done away with, that we should no longer be slaves to sin—because anyone who has died has been set free from sin. Now if we died with Christ, we believe that we will also live with him. For we know that since Christ was raised from the dead, he cannot die again; death no longer has mastery over him. The death he died, he died to sin once for all; but the life he lives, he lives to God. In the same way, count yourselves dead to sin but alive to God in Christ Jesus. Therefore do not let sin reign in your mortal body so that you obey its evil desires. Do not offer any part of your self to sin as an instrument of wickedness, but rather offer yourselves to God as those who have been brought from death to life; and offer every part of yourself to him as an instrument of

righteousness. *For sin shall not be your master, because you are not under law, but under grace.* . . . But thanks be to God that, though you used to be slaves to sin, you have come to obey from your heart the pattern of teaching that has now claimed your allegiance. *You have been set free from sin and have become slaves to righteousness.* (Romans 6:6–14, 17–18)

If we know all this, why do we fail? Why do we walk right back into the sin we've been set free from? There is a world of difference between knowing something and believing something.

The beauty of fasting is that it is such a wonderful catalyst for spiritual change. Like we talked about in chapter 1, we cooperate (mightily) with fasting, but it is God who does the deep transformation, the lasting change. Part of that transformation occurs during the preparation for a fast (confession and forgiveness), and part of the transformation occurs during the fast itself (prayer, meditation, and journaling). However, the biggest changes often come after the fast, when we've weathered the temptations and put into practice the changes made in our souls.

I am learning that this transformation is not made by changing my actions but by changing my mind. Central to my mind is how I think; central to how I think is what I believe. My beliefs have matured because of the truths gleaned in fasting, and my mind and my actions have changed. The rest of this chapter is devoted to sharing how to apply the newfound truths gained by fasting so that we can live obediently and victoriously.

KNOWING ISN'T BELIEVING

When we believe that God loves us, we can trust Him. When we trust Him we obey Him. If we have doubt about God's goodness, we won't trust Him. Until we're convinced of God's unconditional, devoted love for us, we won't trust Him. If we don't trust Him, we won't obey Him.

Stay with me here. The reason we seek to serve another master, to disobey, is a belief problem. When we fall into a pattern of sin, we are believing that God is not trustworthy or loving. We are believing a lie. It is the sin of unbelief. Maybe the lie is that food satisfies, or that we deserve to withhold forgiveness, or that we—not God—know what is best for us. If we believe deep down it is not safe to surrender completely to God, it is because we don't trust Him. We know we should trust, we know He loves us, we know about Jesus and redemption, but we don't believe.

My first reaction when I realized I was slipping back into sin was, "But I know better!" The problem isn't a knowledge problem. We can know a lot, but it's what we believe that matters. I was believing my flesh deserved to be satisfied, when the truth is my flesh needs to be put to death! I was believing God wasn't enough, that I needed God and food. Remember, the devil has not given up the fight. His chief weapon is lies. He lied to Eve (Genesis 3:1–5). Jesus called him the father of all lies (John 8:44). Satan works hard to get us to believe a lie. Why? Because we act according to what we believe, not what we know.

We act (obey or disobey) based on what we believe. If we believe the roads are treacherously icy, we won't drive on them. If we believe the roads are icy but not treacherous, many of us will drive on them. The condition of the road has not changed; our individual beliefs about the condition of the road determine our individual actions. If we believe an amusement ride is too scary, we won't ride it. It doesn't matter that everyone else says it is fun, we won't believe them and we won't ride it. What we believe about God determines how we act. We can say we know that God is all-powerful and that nothing is impossible for Him.

We can sing of God's love. Just because we know something, doesn't mean we believe it.

Belief requires faith. Faith "is confidence in what we hope for and assurance about what we do not see" (Hebrews 11:1). By faith we believe that God loves us. By faith we believe that God is trustworthy. By faith, we obey. The writer of Hebrews addresses unbelief and warns us to "see to it, brothers and sisters, that none of you has a sinful, unbelieving heart that turns away from the living God. But encourage one another daily, as long as it is called 'Today,' so that none of you may be hardened by sin's deceitfulness" (Hebrews 3:12–13).

WE ARE NOT UNAWARE

In addition to being a liar, the devil fights dirty. He will kick you when you are down. If believing a lie deceived you into sin, his next tactic is to convince you that your prior victory was just a fluke, that you'll never overcome this sin. He's a liar! I am convinced the enemy knows that obedience brings victory. Our enemy wants us to be defeated, not victorious. His favorite and most effective lie is that God is not to be believed or trusted. Satan is always looking for any opportunity to sow seeds of doubt in a believer's mind.

Paul, writing about obedience and forgiveness to the church at Corinth, warns that obedience is necessary "in order that Satan might not outwit us. For we are not unaware of his schemes" (2 Corinthians 2:11). Actually, I think Satan has done a very good job of outwitting us and keeping us unaware of his schemes. When he finds something that works, he'll keep using it. Let's look at his first success in making a lie sound believable.

When Satan approached Eve in the garden, everything was perfect: no sin, no disease, no heartache. It was paradise. Adam and Eve were living in a perfect Promised Land. Ah, but there was one thing off limits; God commanded Adam, "You are free to eat from any tree in the garden; but you must not eat from the tree of the knowledge of good and evil, for when you eat from it you will surely die" (Genesis 2:16–17).

Now, let's examine the exchange between the devil and Eve:

Now the serpent was more crafty than any of the wild animals the Lord God had made. He said to the woman, "Did God really say, 'You must not eat from any tree in the garden'?" The woman said to the serpent, "We may eat fruit from the trees in the garden, but God did say, 'You must not eat fruit from the tree that is in the middle of the garden, and you must not touch it, or you will die.'" "You will not certainly die," the serpent said to the woman. "For God knows that when you eat from it your eyes will be opened, and you will be like God, knowing good and evil." When the woman saw that the fruit of the tree was good for food and pleasing to the eye, and also desirable for gaining wisdom, she took some and ate it. She also gave some to her husband, who was with her, and he ate it. (Genesis 3:1–6)

The first scheme the devil uses is to engage in conversation. He starts a whole dialogue and maneuvers Eve into defending God— "Did God say . . . ?" Eve, perhaps defensively, replies that she can eat of the trees in the garden. Then she adds, "But God did say, 'You must not eat fruit from the tree that is in the middle of the garden, and you must not touch it, or you will die.'" Notice, she does not call it by name, the tree of the knowledge of good and evil, and she also adds something God never said—death comes from not just eating its fruit but merely touching it.

The second, very effective, scheme the devil uses is to cast doubt. He's subtle: "Really, Eve, you must have misunderstood. Surely you will not die! That can't be what God really said."

The third scheme, especially effective once doubt is in place, is to suggest that God is withholding something wonderful. The devil insinuates that God can't really be trusted or believed because He is keeping you from having all the good things you should have. No, more than that—all the wonderful things you deserve.

NOT OUTWITTED

Being aware of the devil's schemes keeps us from being outwitted. Eve was outwitted. We need not be.

The first scheme was starting a conversation. Here's how we handle this one: Don't answer! I grew up outside of New York City and went into Manhattan regularly. By the time I was sixteen, I would ride the Long Island Railroad to Penn Station with my friends on most Saturdays. I was taught to ignore strangers and never talk to them. I was taught to keep my eyes to myself; never make eye contact with strangers (everyone knows that in New York City only psychos and con men try to make eye contact). When you're walking in Manhattan as a sixteen-year-old, this was good advice. When I got married, my husband and I were stationed in Virginia. There I met girls from Arkansas, South Carolina, and Georgia—nice, sweet Southern girls. The idea of ignoring people was foreign to them!

I think most Christian women are like those sweet Southern girls. We speak when spoken to. Stop it! Don't give the devil the time of day. Do not talk to him. Don't argue with him; don't defend your faith, yourself, or your God. Run right to God: "Submit yourselves, then, to God. Resist the devil, and he will flee from you" (James 4:7).

The devil's second scheme was casting doubt. If you ever hear yourself thinking, *Did God really say . . . ?* consider yourself invited to a Doubt Party. This is how Satan twists truth. He doesn't come at the truth head on, he comes sideways. Remember his temptations of Jesus; He used *Scripture!* The devil takes a truth and adds a little lie and makes it sound good. If it sounded evil, most believers would recognize the lie. Instead, he deceives; he doesn't want us to recognize the lie. If we believe the lie, we'll act accordingly.

The third scheme was to malign God. Again, the devil did not stand up and shout, "God is a liar! God doesn't care! God is keeping all the good things for himself!" Using our flesh nature, our natural desire to be our own boss (our own god), he makes us feel deprived. If Eve could have felt deprived in Paradise, we can certainly feel deprived in this world. The root of this lie is that we could do a better job of running our lives and providing for ourselves than God can. It demotes the Holy, sovereign, loving God to a fickle taskmaster.

BELIEVING THE TRUTH

The reason the enemy is so effective with his lies is that we don't always recognize them as lies. Did you know that the Secret Service, the ones who protect the president, was formed in 1865 under the Department of the Treasury?[2] Back then, their main mission and focus was detecting counterfeit money. To this day, agents are trained in counterfeit money identification. You might have heard how they are trained. For hours at a time, they touch, see, smell, and handle only genuine United States currency. Then, when a counterfeit bill is slipped in, they immediately spot it. They know what is wrong because they know what is right. We need to do the same thing. The more we know God through His Word, the faster we will spot the lies of the enemy. The more truth we know, the faster we will discern a lie.

Often the enemy will use our emotions to lie to us. If we don't feel forgiven, maybe we aren't really forgiven. If we don't feel loved, maybe it's because we're not loved. If we don't feel worthy, maybe it's because we're worthless. If we feel ashamed, maybe we are condemned. Oh, the devious and cunning schemes of the devil! We can't live by feelings; we must live by faith.

The feelings may be real, but that doesn't make them true. To live by faith, we must be sure of what we believe. We must believe the truth of Scripture. We must fight feelings and deception with truth.

Remember the devil's first scheme? Starting a conversation? How often do random thoughts pop into our heads? How many running conversations do we keep in our mind all day long? Our first line of defense is our minds. We can choose what we allow to dwell in our thoughts. Yes, sometimes false thoughts do pop in, but we don't need to make them comfortable and invite them to stay. Paul teaches us what to do with the arguments and pretensions (another way of saying deceptions) that the enemy uses all the time:

> For though we live in the world, we do not wage war as the world does. The weapons we fight with are not the weapons of the world. On the contrary, they have divine power to demolish strongholds. We demolish arguments and every pretension that sets itself up against the knowledge of God, *and we take captive every thought to make it obedient to Christ.* (2 Corinthians 10:3–5)

Take every thought captive to the obedience of Christ. That is, examine every thought in light of the truth of Jesus and the Word of God. If it doesn't match what God says, throw it out! Treat the thought like the thief that it is. "Do not conform to the pattern of this world, but be transformed by the renewing of your mind" (Romans 12:2). We renew our minds by determining what occupies our minds.

How do we take every thought captive and renew our minds?

The first step is to pray. Ask God for help. Sometimes I'm not sure what is bothering me so I pray and ask God to show me the emotion or the lie. I love the Amplified Bible version of Psalm 139:23–24: "Search me [thoroughly], God, and know my heart; test me and know my anxious thoughts. See if there is any offensive way in me, and lead me in the way everlasting." Then, take a moment and become fully aware of what is in your mind. Examine the thought or feeling in light of God's Word. Is it true? If it is false, the second step is a decision. Will we stop thinking about and dwelling on this thought or emotion? We must choose. When we choose not to be consumed by the patterns of this world and the lies of the enemy for one more minute, we are ready to renew our minds.

The third step, renewing our minds, is to replace the thought or negative emotion with the truth of God's Word. It's no good to try to stop thinking about something—it's like when someone tells you not to think about a pink elephant. Of course, your mind now has a vivid picture of a pink elephant. No, we must exchange the lie for the truth. If you can't think of one verse of Scripture, sing a praise song or a hymn. Sing, "Jesus loves me this I know, for the Bible tells me so." Be intentional; put a new, good, and true thought in your mind. Focus on this truth. Repeat these steps, prayerfully, until your mind is renewed.

The power of this practice is that we are doing more than conforming our mind to God's Word, we are choosing what we believe. Since we act according to what we believe, this practice is our path to obedience. And obedience is the key to victory—the victorious, overcoming life that we long for.

The intense time you spent in the Word and in prayer during your fast will come back to bless you one hundredfold. The verses you wrote in your journal, the verses you meditated on, the verses you memorized, and the time you spent reading God's Word have equipped you to defeat the enemy and his lies.

WELL DEFENDED

Many of us are familiar with the passage in Ephesians that describes the armor of God:

> Finally, be strong in the Lord and in his mighty power. Put on the full armor of God, so that you can take your stand against the devil's schemes. For our struggle is not against flesh and blood, but against the rulers, against the authorities, against the powers of this dark world and against the spiritual forces of evil in the heavenly realms. Therefore put on the full armor of God, so that when the day of evil comes, you may be able to stand your ground, and after you have done everything, to stand. Stand firm then, with the belt of truth buckled around your waist, with the breastplate of righteousness in place, and with your feet fitted with the readiness that comes from the gospel of peace. In addition to all this, take up the shield of faith, with which you can extinguish all the flaming arrows of the evil one. Take the helmet of salvation and the sword of the Spirit, which is the word of God. And pray in the Spirit on all occasions with all kinds of prayers and requests. With this in mind, be alert and always keep on praying for all the Lord's people. (Ephesians 6:10–18)

Not long ago, when I read this passage, the word *stand* just kept leaping off the page. It was one of those "God is speaking through His Word to me" moments. I went back and reread the passage. The word *stand* is used five times in these eight verses. I knew that was significant. Then, immediately, another verse came to mind. I remembered the verse about being still, that the Lord would do the fighting. I looked it up and was struck again by the word *stand*.

The verse is from Exodus, and it's after the Israelites have left Egypt and Pharaoh is coming out to attack them. And here's what Moses says, "Do not be afraid. *Stand firm* and you will see the deliverance the Lord will bring you today. The Egyptians you see today you will never see again. *The Lord will fight for you; you need only be still*" (Exodus 14:13–14).

Stand. Stand your ground. Stand firm. Be still. Wait a minute, what about fighting the fight? What about the battle? In both passages, it's not we who fight—it's the Lord who fights for us. We need only to stand firm. Look again at the Ephesians passage. All of the armor is defensive except for the sword of the Spirit, which is the Word of God—the only offensive weapon we have. Notice one other thing: The breastplate of righteousness and the shield of faith (believing!) protect only the front of the body. God has got our backs.

When we incorporate the discipline of fasting into our walk with Christ, we start to truly appreciate "that man does not live on bread alone but on every word that comes from the mouth of the Lord" (Deuteronomy 8:3). We learn to live the Word—

to believe it,

to recognize when the enemy twists it,

to obey its truth,

to walk in victory,

to stand firm and watch God deliver us from our enemy!

WALK BY FAITH OR STAND BY GRACE?

Should we walk by faith or stand by grace? Both. We choose what to believe. The disciplines help us to trust and believe everything that God says about himself is trustworthy, true, and reliable. That's the walk. Then we go one step further and stand firm, trusting that God is able. And more than that, believing God is good, even when life is not.

We walk out our faith, we put into action what we believe and obey. We do all of this to the extent that we really believe we are dead to the sin nature and we now live hidden with Christ in God (Colossians 3:3). This is the essence of grace. The danger of the law is that the focus is forever on us, not God. The focus, under law, is on what we've done or not done. The law promotes self-righteousness, which leads to spiritual defeat. There is no standing firm and watching God under law—it's all about self.

John's gospel declares, "The law was given through Moses: grace and truth came through Jesus Christ" (John 1:17). Our disciplines, and fasting in particular, are not laws to follow; they are ways to live in grace and truth. Jesus came full of grace and truth. His obedience flowed from that. He was never earning His way into God's favor; He already had God's favor and He knew it. So do we! But do we believe it?

THE HARVEST IS RIPE

When Jesus was with the woman at the well, the disciples came back and encouraged Him to eat.

> But he said to them, "I have food to eat that you know nothing about." Then his disciples said to each other, "Could some- one have brought him food?" "My food," said Jesus, "is to

do the will of him who sent me and to finish his work. Don't you have a saying, 'It's still four months until harvest'? I tell you, open your eyes and look at the fields! They are ripe for harvest" (John 4:32–35).

We are not transformed to live victoriously as overcomers, walking by faith and not by sight, so that we can feel good about ourselves. We are "a chosen people, a royal priesthood, a holy nation, God's special possession, that you may declare the praises of him who called you out of darkness into his wonderful light. Once you were not a people, but now you are the people of God; once you had not received mercy, but now you have received mercy." Peter goes on to exhort us, "Dear friends, I urge you, as foreigners and exiles, to abstain from sinful desires, which wage war against your soul. Live such good lives among the pagans that, though they accuse you of doing wrong, they may see your good deeds and glorify God on the day he visits us" (1 Peter 2:9–12).

Fasting and the other disciplines are the tools God uses to work His will into our lives—for it is God who works in you to will and to act according to His good purpose (Philippians 2:13). When we do His will, when we obey Him, we bring Him glory. We can't glorify God in our natural, selfish state; we must be changed. The disciplines help us in this transformation, this change from self-centered to God-centered. That's the real goal of our lives, to glorify God—not to be good at fasting or praying or meditating or journaling or walking or standing.

As we are transformed, as we are able to glorify and magnify God, the world sees this. We can live our lives in such a way that even the lost would praise God and be saved, for Jesus says, "Let your light shine before others, that they may see your good deeds and praise your Father in heaven" (Matthew 5:16).

The harvest is ripe.

CHAPTER 7

Preventing Fasting Fiascos

Why, my soul, are you downcast? Why so disturbed within me? Put your hope in God, for I will yet praise him, my Savior and my God.
—*Psalm 42:5*

Okay. Maybe the fast didn't go as planned. You ended it before the day (or week or month) was done. Maybe you feel like you've failed. Maybe you finished the fast and you hated every minute of it. You were hungry, you had a headache, and you were cranky. Maybe you tried fasting a while ago, had a horrible experience, and now you're wondering if you can ever fast successfully.

Really? You've always practiced every other spiritual discipline perfectly? Never missed a day of prayer? Never missed a day in the Word? Always tithed faithfully and cheerfully? So, did you just give up ever trying to practice those disciplines again? Never picked up the Bible again because you neglected it for a week? Never prayed again? Or tithed?

What if fasting really is just another tool in the pursuit of grace and the transformed life? What if it's something you can learn? What if a stumble or even a series of failures means . . . absolutely nothing! What if fasting truly is just the means to an end? What if the end—a transformed, overcoming, victorious Christian life—is yet within your reach?

As I shared earlier, I finished my first forty-day juice and water fast in 1999. In June 2000, I sensed the Lord calling me to fast for twenty-one days. *Piece of cake!* I thought. *Only half the time of my last long fast.* As I prayed, I heard that the fast should start on July 5. So far, so good. Then on June 18 (I only know these dates because of my journals—just another plug for keeping a prayer journal!), I got the bright idea that I would start my fast early. Why? God's idea wasn't good enough? Anyway, off I started with little preparation—other than my reason to fast (to die to self and seek God's righteousness) and the verse from Galatians 2:20: "I have been crucified with Christ and I no longer live, but Christ lives in me. The life I now live in the body, I live by faith in the Son of God who loved me and gave himself for me."

In addition to this poor preparation, I was in the middle of teaching administrative law as an adjunct professor, moving out of my house for a weekend so a friend could use it for a Bible study reunion, and my children were three and five years old. And out of school for the summer. Oh, and I was potty-training my three-year-old. By the second day, I had a migraine headache that was so bad I was throwing up. Then the diarrhea started. I can hardly describe how horrible I felt. Yet, in my pig-headed way, I was determined to fast. Fortunately, I have a wonderful husband who, with great concern, asked, "Is this really the best time to fast? Don't you have a lot going on?" Then he flat out asked me to stop the fast. I stopped the fast. By the next morning I was completely restored.

Set Up to Fail

I failed at fasting. Spectacularly. It was time to sit down with the Lord and reassess this whole fasting thing. In His gentle way, He opened my eyes to why it didn't go well:

1. I moved the date God had given me. As if I know more than God about when to undertake an extended fast?!
2. I did not properly prepare, especially physically.
3. I did not slow down and rest during the first days of the fast. Worse yet, I became dehydrated.
4. I was full of pride. Remember that "piece of cake" thought? Fasting is hard. Somehow I thought I was immune to the difficulties of fasting because I had successfully fasted for forty days.
5. More pride. I forgot that fasting for more than a day is a call from God himself, not just a bright idea of mine. I stupidly thought I could fast in my own strength.

Thankfully the Lord showed me this failure wasn't forever. Every single thing that contributed to it could have been avoided. I learned much about the grace of God in this experience. After I confessed my pride and self-sufficiency and received God's complete forgiveness, I had no doubt that I could and would fast again. Still, it's helpful to break down everything that went wrong.

First, I changed the dates of the fast. Or perhaps more accurately, I disobeyed God; let's just call it what it is. I don't think I can emphasize enough that fasting for more than twenty-four hours is a serious undertaking. A call to fast is specific, not general. Just as we talked about in chapter 4, when we are called to fast, we need to ask God what kind of a fast, for how long, and for what reason. When God appoints a time, He means it.

One of my favorite stories about fasting and God's perfect timing is in the book of Esther. Esther was a beautiful Jewish girl who was selected to be the King of Persia's queen, after his first queen dishonored him. She kept the fact that she was Jewish quiet. While Esther was queen, one of the king's advisors, Haman, was insulted when Mordecai (the relative who raised Esther) refused to kneel before him. This enraged Haman and he convinced the king to make an official proclamation: "Dispatches were sent by couriers to all the king's provinces with the order to destroy, kill and annihilate all the Jews—young and old, women and children—on a single day, the thirteenth day of the twelfth month, the month of Adar, and to plunder their goods" (Esther 3:13).

Mordecai was, of course, devastated when he heard this news. Esther, unaware of the proclamation, sent a servant, Hathach, to find out what was upsetting Mordecai. Mordecai told Hathach to urge Esther to "go into the king's presence to beg for mercy and plead with him for her people" (Esther 4:8). So,

> Hathak went back and reported to Esther what Mordecai had said. Then she instructed him to say to Mordecai, "All the king's officials and the people of the royal provinces know that for any man or woman who approaches the king in the inner court without being summoned the king has but one law: that they be put to death unless the king extends the gold scepter to them and spares their lives. But thirty days have passed since I was called to go to the king." When Esther's words were reported to Mordecai, he sent back this answer: "Do not think that because you are in the king's house you alone of all the Jews will escape. For if you remain silent at this time, relief and deliverance for the Jews will arise from another place, but you and your father's family will perish. *And who knows but that you have come to your royal position for such a time as this?*" Then Esther sent this reply to Mordecai: "Go,

gather together all the Jews who are in Susa, and fast for me. Do not eat or drink for three days, night or day. I and my attendants will fast as you do. When this is done, I will go to the king, even though it is against the law. And if I perish, I perish" (Esther 4:9–16).

For such a time as this. I am convinced that our times are in God's hands. We were intentionally created to live in a specific time to do the works God prepared, in advance, for us to do (Psalm 139:13–16; Ephesians 2:10). Esther was exactly where she needed to be, when she needed to be there, for God's will to be done. Her fast was perfectly timed and the results were nothing short of astounding.

After Esther was admitted into the king's presence, she throws banquets for the king and Haman. At the second banquet, she reveals that she is a Jew and that Haman's plot would include her. Haman pleads with her "and was falling on the couch where Esther was reclining," and the king sees this. The king accuses Haman of molesting his queen. Watch what happens: Haman is hanged on the very gallows he had built to hang Mordecai on; Esther is given Haman's estate; Mordecai is promoted to the highest rank, just below the king himself; and a new edict was issued that allowed the Jews to defend themselves against the first proclamation, whereby they killed their enemies instead of being killed!

My second mistake was being so focused on the spiritual component of my fast (oh, the lofty goal of dying to self!) that I completely neglected the physical side—with disastrous results.

As I have emphasized throughout this book, fasting has both a spiritual and a physical component. You must do both together. The best spiritual intentions in fasting are useless without adequate physical preparation.

This fast was taking place in June in Kansas. Have you been to Kansas in June? It is unbelievably hot. One reason I got the migraine headache that started the whole cascade of misery is that I did not drink enough. When you're not eating, you are not getting the liquid that's found in food. When you're fasting, you must increase your liquid intake. When you're fasting *and* dealing with hot weather, you must really increase your liquid intake.

The third thing I did wrong was not slowing down and resting enough.

Part of the reason I failed to do the most basic thing in fasting—drink more—was that I was too busy. Huge mistake, both physically and spiritually. The point of fasting is not to give up food. The point of fasting is to pursue God with single-mindedness. I missed that point and paid for it. When we are fasting for ANY amount of time, we must schedule downtime. That is, lying down and resting quietly. It's not adding a little extra prayer time, or skipping a social invitation. If I can't lie down in the day, I plan on being in bed early. By early, I mean by 8 p.m.

Perhaps the reason that fasting is such a powerful tool for spiritual growth and maturity, is that you can't just add it on top of an already busy life. Fasting forces you to slow down. Fasting forces you to examine yourself and your actions in a way that no other spiritual discipline does.

The fourth mistake I made was being prideful based on a past success.

You would think that after a forty-day fast I might have gained a little humility and conquered some pride. Evidently not. In fact, because I had finished a forty-day fast that was nothing less than life-transforming, I thought I had this whole fasting thing down pat. It was this sin of pride that allowed me to walk into a twenty-one-day fast woefully unprepared. Not just the physical lack of preparation, but assuming I could change the timing of the fast—all a result of pride. As soon as I stopped throwing up, I confessed and repented. I'd love to tell you that pride is no longer an issue in my life, but that's not true. I will tell you that I am much quicker at recognizing pride and not falling into its trap. Fasting, and this failure specifically, taught me more about the sin of pride than years of Bible study.

The fifth thing I did wrong was to rely on my own strength, trying to be self-sufficient.

As plainly as I can, let me just say you can NEVER fast in your own strength. In fact, it can't even be called a fast if you're trying to fast in your own strength. Fasting in our own strength is not a response to God's call and His work in our lives; it is a misguided attempt to make ourselves right in God's eyes. That's law, not grace. I believe it is not only foolish but dangerous.

Fasting for the best of intentions, but without the call of Christ, is doomed to fail. As we talked about in chapter 6, when Jesus fasted for forty days (Matthew 3:16–4:1; Luke 3:21–4:13), it was at the beginning of His ministry. A well-meaning Christian could look at these passages and determine that a great way to start, or jump-start, a ministry would be with a forty-day fast. Yet it was not Jesus' idea to fast. He was called specifically ("led by the Spirit") to enter the desert and fast. Undertaking an extended fast, without the Spirit's leading, could open the door to serious physical, spiritual, and mental consequences.

Extended fasting without the call to fast is not true fasting, it is sin. Proverbs 5:21–23 states, "For your ways are in full view of the Lord, and he examines all your paths. The evil deeds of the wicked ensnare them; the cords of their sins hold them fast. For lack of discipline they will die, *led astray by their own great folly.*"

Not eating for weeks at a time in our own strength, because of our own desires, is folly, no matter how we might disguise those desires with spiritual words of self-sacrifice ("I'm dying to self!" "I'm seeking increase in ministry!" "I'm interceding for the lost!"). The root sin here is self-glorification. It is the opposite of the true humility of a God-centered and God-called fast. We are wise to be aware of this trap. Daniel 3–4 gives us a stunning picture of the consequences of self-glorification in the account of King Nebuchadnezzar.

Nebuchadnezzar was the king of a vast empire and was used by God in the judgment of Israel and the fall of Jerusalem. One example of his pride and self-glorification is the famous story of Shadrach, Meshach, and Abednego. The reason they were thrown into the fiery furnace, and then rescued by God, was because they refused to worship Nebuchadnezzar. King Nebuchadnezzar glorified himself with an image made in gold, ninety feet high by nine feet wide, and demanded that every person fall down and worship it on command.

Later on, the king had a dream, which Daniel was summoned to interpret. He tells the king:

> You will be driven away from people and will live with the wild animals; you will eat grass like the ox and be drenched with the dew of heaven. Seven times will pass by for you until you acknowledge that the Most High is sovereign over all kingdoms on earth and gives them to anyone he wishes. . . . Your kingdom will be restored to you when you acknowledge that Heaven rules. Therefore, Your Majesty, be pleased to accept my advice: Renounce your sins by doing what is right, and your wickedness by being kind to the oppressed. It may be that then your prosperity will continue. (Daniel 4:25–27)

King Nebuchadnezzar does not repent of his pride. Scripture records his great arrogance: "Twelve months later, as the king was walking on the roof of the royal palace of Babylon, he said, 'Is not this the great Babylon I have built as the royal residence, by my mighty power and for the glory of my majesty?'" (Daniel 4:29–30). Even after being warned in a dream, Nebuchadnezzar still believes it was his own strength, his own glory that mattered.

Not surprisingly, all of God's judgments come to pass. The king is essentially insane and lives among the beasts of the field for seven years. Talk about a humbling experience. Nebuchadnezzar lost everything as a result of his pride and self-glory. Yet, after God humbled him, Nebuchadnezzar was reestablished:

> At the end of that time, I, Nebuchadnezzar, raised my eyes toward heaven, and my sanity was restored. Then I praised the Most High; I honored and glorified him who lives forever. His dominion is an eternal dominion; his kingdom endures from generation to generation. All the peoples of the earth are regarded as nothing. He does as he pleases with the powers of heaven and the peoples of the earth. No one can hold back his hand or say to him: "What have you done?" At the same time that my sanity was restored, my honor and splendor were returned to me for the glory of my kingdom. My advisers and nobles sought me out, and I was restored to my throne and became even greater than before. Now I, Nebuchadnezzar, praise and exalt and glorify the King of heaven, because everything he does is right and all his ways are just. *And those who walk in pride he is able to humble.* (Daniel 4:34–37)

I share this biblical example to emphasize that fasting is all about God's glory. There seems to be a slippery slope from self-sufficiency to self-serving to self-glorification. Self-glorification is just another way of saying self-worship. The truth is, any spiritual discipline can be self-serving, a basis for boasting:

Prayer—"I wake at 4 a.m. and pray every morning for hours!"

Giving—"I tithe 20 percent of all I have!"

Serving—"I single-handedly built the new Sunday school wing!"

Study—"I have memorized five hundred Bible verses!"

Fasting—"I have fasted for ___hours/days/weeks!"

Whenever we take our eyes off Jesus, we're in danger of self-glorification. Fasting can be a particular type of self-worship ("Look at my self-control!" "Look at my spirituality!"). Learn from Nebuchadnezzar. Don't walk; run from this lie. Let me say again, fasting is merely the means, not the end. Jesus is the end. Let us worship only Him.

CHAPTER 8

The Sacrifice of Praise

What if you obeyed the call, fasted in the center of God's will, waited for that mountaintop experience . . . and it never came? You keep hearing about how wonderful this fasting stuff is supposed to be and you feel like it never happened for you. Maybe you were counting down the minutes until the next meal or the twenty-fourth hour, all the while thinking, *never again.*

Sometimes fasting, like the other disciplines, is like that. It doesn't mean you did anything wrong. Your fast was as good as anyone else's. Fasting is a sacrifice. Sacrifice is not easy and its benefits are not always immediately obvious. One of the hidden benefits of fasting is that it teaches us to live sacrificially. Richard Foster, in *Celebration of Discipline,*[1] quotes from Elizabeth O'Connor's *Search for Silence.* She had committed to fast for twenty-four hours each week for two years. He notes "the progression from the superficial aspects of fasting toward the deeper rewards" in her observations:

1. I felt it a great accomplishment to go a whole day without food. Congratulated myself on the fact that I found it so easy.

2. Began to see that the above was hardly the goal of fasting. Was helped in this by beginning to feel hunger . . .

3. Began to relate the food fast to other areas of my life where I was more compulsive . . . I did not have to have a seat on the bus to be contented, or to be cool in the summer and warm when it was cold.

4. Reflected more on Christ's suffering and the suffering of those who are hungry and have hungry babies.

5. Six months after beginning the fast discipline, I began to see why a two-year period has been suggested. The experience changes along the way. Hunger on fast days became acute, and the temptation to eat stronger. For the first time I was using the day to find God's will for my life. Began to think about what it meant to *surrender* one's life.

6. I now know that prayer and fasting must be intricately bound together. There is no other way, and yet that way is not yet combined in me.

As difficult as your fast may have been, prayerfully consider pursuing the discipline of fasting for a period of time. Give yourself the opportunity to experience the self-sacrifice of fasting. Perhaps your fast is a sacrifice of praise—your determination to praise God despite how you felt during or after the fast.

Although sacrifice by itself is nothing, sacrifice that teaches us to be God-focused instead of self-focused is everything. A God-centered life is the essence of a life of worship.

True Worship

The timeless Westminster Catechism starts with, "The chief end of man is to glorify [worship] God, and to enjoy him forever."[2] Today we might use the words *most important, primary, paramount,* or *highest* for the word *chief.* The most important thing for believers to do is to worship God. That is as true today as when the Westminster Assembly met in 1649. The apostle John records Jesus' description of true worshipers: "A time is coming and has now come when the true worshipers will worship the Father in spirit and in truth, for they are the kind of worshipers the Father seeks. God is spirit, and his worshipers must worship in the Spirit and in truth" (John 4:23–24). Sometimes worshiping in spirit and truth includes sacrifice.

The intersection of sacrifice and worship is expressed in Paul's letter to the Romans: "Therefore, I urge you, brothers and sisters, in view of God's mercy, to offer your bodies as a *living sacrifice, holy and pleasing to God—this is your true and proper worship*" (Romans 12:1). Peter writes of spiritual sacrifice as the building block of our faith: "As you come to him, the living Stone—rejected by humans but chosen by God and precious to him—you also, like living stones, are being built into a spiritual house to be a holy priesthood, offering spiritual sacrifices acceptable to God through Jesus Christ" (1 Peter 2:4–5). David writes that the humility from "a broken spirit; a broken and contrite heart" is an acceptable spiritual sacrifice (Psalm 51:17). This discipline of fasting is both a teacher of sacrificial living as well as a spiritual sacrifice by itself. When we offer our bodies as living sacrifices, we are worshiping God; we are living a life worthy of the Lord.

WORTHY OF THE CALL

When we cooperate with God and practice the disciplines of faith, we will be changed. The Bible calls it sanctification, the process of being made holy. As much as we desire to be transformed and live the overcoming, victorious life that results from obedience, the real jewel in our crown is to live as Paul describes:

For this reason, since the day we heard about you, we have not stopped praying for you. We continually ask God to fill you with the knowledge of his will through all the wisdom and understanding that the Spirit gives, so that you may live a life worthy of the Lord and please him in every way: bearing fruit in every good work, growing in the knowledge of God, being strengthened with all power according to his glorious might so that you may have great endurance and patience, and giving joyful thanks to the Father, who has qualified you to share in the inheritance of his holy people in the kingdom of light. For he has rescued us from the dominion of darkness and brought us into the kingdom of the Son he loves, in whom we have redemption, the forgiveness of sins. (Colossians 1:9–14)

Believers are called to live a life worthy of God. When we've fasted and there seems to be no outward result, will we trust that God is working on the inside? Will we believe that God is sanctifying our souls?

PERSEVERE

Maybe we've fasted with a specific prayer request, and at the end of the fast, there seems to be no answer to that prayer. Jesus tells us to keep asking. Right after He taught the disciples the Lord's Prayer, He told them,

Suppose you have a friend, and you go to him at midnight and say, "Friend, lend me three loaves of bread; a friend of mine on a journey has come to me, and I have no food to offer him." And suppose the one inside answers, "Don't bother me. The door is already locked, and my children and I are in bed. I can't get up and give you anything." I tell you, even though he will not get up and give you the bread because of friendship, yet because of your shameless audacity he will surely get up and give you as much as you need.

So I say to you: Ask and it will be given to you; seek and you will find; knock and the door will be opened to you. For everyone who asks receives; the one who seeks finds; and the one who knocks, the door will be opened.

Which of you fathers, if your son asks for a fish, will give him a snake instead? Or if he asks for an egg, will give him a scorpion? If you then, though you are evil, know how to give good gifts to your children, how much more will your Father in heaven give the Holy Spirit to those who ask him! (Luke 11:5–13)

What is *your* persistent prayer?

A Final Word

Whether you are a veteran faster or are just beginning to include fasting in your life, please know that I am praying for you. I believe God will bless you through this ancient yet timely spiritual discipline. I am praying that your faith will increase beyond measure and I am "confident...that he who began a good work in you will carry it on to completion until the day of Christ Jesus" (Philippians 1:6). Be encouraged. I rejoice, in advance, with you in your fasting victories!

Acknowledgments

Where else to start but to acknowledge the great gift of salvation in Jesus Christ. Amen.

Thank you, Mom and Dad, for your love and support all my life. Thank you, John, the love of my life and my best friend, for your amazing encouragement. You are the least surprised that this book is written. Clare and Andrew, the best kids in the world and the joy of my heart, thank you for your patience and faith in me.

Thank you, friends, for reading the proposal, praying for me, and asking—well, sometimes nagging—"How's the book coming along?" Each of you is a blessing from God: Judy, Brenda, Shellie, Merial, Karen, Claudia, Audrey, Rebecca, Christina, Julie, Molly (now in glory with Jesus), Lynn, Amanda, Nancy, Sheryl, Lisa, and Sandy. If I had a fan club, Sandy would be president.

Thank you, Bethany House, and especially Jeff Braun, for taking a chance on this first-time author. Jeff saw the promise of this book and took me by the hand from proposal to manuscript. You, sir, are a prince among men.

Notes

Chapter 1. What Is Fasting?

1. Richard J. Foster, *Celebration of Discipline: The Path to Spiritual Growth,* Richard J. Foster (San Francisco: HarperSanFrancisco, 2003).

2. An excellent discussion of the disciplines is in Richard Foster's *Celebration of Discipline,* and in Mark Buchanan's *Your God Is Too Safe* (Sisters, OR: Multnomah Publishers, 2001).

Chapter 2. Why Fast?

1. One of the best books on the spiritual benefits and reasons to fast is John Piper's *A Hunger for God* (Wheaton, IL: Crossway Books, 1997).

2. "It's Me, O Lord, Standing in the Need of Prayer" is a traditional gospel song. The author is unknown.

3. R. C. Sproul, *Pleasing God* (Carol Stream, IL: Tyndale House, 1988).

Chapter 3. Should *You* Fast?

1. Don Colbert, *Fasting Made Easy* (Lake Mary, FL: Siloam, 2004), 41–42.

2. Jerry Falwell and Elmer Towns, eds., *Fasting Can Change Your Life* (Ventura, CA: Regal Books, 1998), 89–94.

3. Larry Crabb, *The PAPA Prayer* (Nashville: Thomas Nelson, 2007), 17.

4. Oswald Chambers, *My Utmost for His Highest* (Uhlrichsville, OH: Barbour, 1997), June 8 entry.

5. Piper, *A Hunger for God,* 175.

Chapter 4. Getting Ready to Fast

1. Mark Buchanan, *Your God Is Too Safe* (Sisters, OR: Multnomah Publishers, 2001), 189.

2. Stormie Omartian, *The Power of a Praying Nation* (Eugene, OR: Harvest House, 2002), 9–10.

Chapter 5. (en)During the Fast

1. Richard J. Foster, *Celebration of Discipline* (New York: Harper and Row, 1978), 48.

2. Dallas Willard, *The Spirit of the Disciplines* (New York: Harper One, 1990), 167.

3. The Campus Crusade for Christ Web site has a fasting schedule and broth recipes that are excellent. *www.ccci.org.*

4. Willard, 167.

5. Kathryn Scott, "Hungry (Falling on My Knees)," *Satisfy*, Integrity/Columbia Records, 2003.

6. Richard J. Foster, Ed., *The Renovaré Spiritual Formation Bible*, NRSV (San Francisco: HarperSanFrancisco, 2005), 2301. This Bible has a Spiritual Disciplines Index compiled by Dallas Willard, and meditation is included in the index.

7. Sarah Young, *Jesus Calling: Enjoying Peace in His Presence* (Nashville: Thomas Nelson, 2004), August 2 entry.

8. "Trust and Obey," Text by John H. Sammis, 1846–1919; music by Daniel B. Towner, 1850–1919.

Chapter 6. You Did It!

1. Don Colbert, *Fasting Made Easy* (Lake Mary, FL: Siloam, 2004), 86.

2. The Secret Service is now part of the Department of Homeland Security. Its role was expanded to include protecting the president after the assassination of President McKinley in 1901.

Chapter 8. The Sacrifice of Praise

1. Richard J. Foster, *Celebration of Discipline* (New York: Harper and Row, 1978), 50 and endnote 10.

2. The Westminster Shorter Catechism, Question #1: "What is the chief end of man? Man's chief end is to glorify God, and to enjoy him forever" (1 Corinthians 10:31; Romans 11:36; Psalm 73:25–28).

Bibliography/Resource List

Blackaby, Henry. *Experiencing God: Knowing and Doing the Will of God* (workbook). Nashville: LifeWay Press, 1990.

Bright, Bill. *The Coming Revival: America's Call to Fast, Pray, and "Seek God's Face."* Orlando, FL: New Life Publications, 1995.

Colbert, Don. *Fasting Made Easy.* Lake Mary, FL: Siloam, 2004.

Falwell, Jerry, and Elmer L. Towns. *Fasting Can Change Your Life.* Ventura, CA: Regal, 1998.

Foster, Richard J. *Celebration of Discipline: The Path to Spiritual Growth.* San Francisco: Harper & Row, 1978.

Franklin, Jentezen. *Fasting.* Lake Mary, FL: Charisma House, 2008.

Hickey, Marilyn. *The Power of Prayer and Fasting.* New York: Warner Faith, 2006.

Piper, John. *A Hunger for God: Desiring God through Fasting and Prayer.* Wheaton, IL: Crossway, 1997.

Towns, Elmer L. *Fasting for Spiritual Breakthrough.* Ventura, CA: Regal, 1996.

Willard, Dallas. *The Spirit of the Disciplines: Understanding How God Changes Lives.* San Francisco: HarperSanFrancisco, 1988.

About the Author

Lisa Nelson completed her first forty-day fast in 1999. It was nothing less than life-changing. Since then, she has led retreats and workshops on all types of fasts, equipping and encouraging others in this Christian discipline. An active speaker and leader in an international ministry to military spouses, Protestant Women of the Chapel, Lisa holds a juris doctor (JD) degree from Washington College of Law and served as an army Judge Advocate General (JAG) Corps officer and a special assistant United States attorney. She has also been an adjunct professor, teaching constitutional law and business law.

Lisa and her husband, John, a colonel in the United States Army, are the proud parents of two children. A native of Long Island, New York, Lisa has lived on three continents and now resides in Fairfax, Virginia (in her eighteenth home).

For more information, visit www.awomansguide.org.